D0195471

Wildly
OPTIMISTIC

Other products by Al Carraway

More than the Tattooed Mormon

Cheers to Eternity!

Rooted—scripture journal

You've Got This!—contributor

With God Life Is Oh So Good—journal

Set Goals. Say Prayers. Work Hard—journal

I Know—journal

AL CARRAWAY

Best-Selling Author of *More than the Tattooed Mormon*

OPTIMISTIC

GAINING NEW PERSPECTIVE
FOR LIFE'S CHALLENGES

CFI

AN IMPRINT OF CEDAR FORT, INC.
SPRINGVILLE, UTAH

© 2019 Al Carraway

All rights reserved.

No part of this book may be reproduced in any form whatsoever, whether by graphic, visual, electronic, film, microfilm, tape recording, or any other means, without prior written permission of the publisher, except in the case of brief passages embodied in critical reviews and articles.

This is not an official publication of The Church of Jesus Christ of Latter-day Saints. The opinions and views expressed herein belong solely to the author and do not necessarily represent the opinions or views of Cedar Fort, Inc. Permission for the use of sources, graphics, and photos is also solely the responsibility of the author.

ISBN 13: 978-1-4621-2338-4

Published by CFI, an imprint of Cedar Fort, Inc.
2373 W. 700 S., Springville, UT 84663
Distributed by Cedar Fort, Inc., www.cedarfort.com

Library of Congress Control Number: 2019947926

Cover design by Shawnda T. Craig
Cover design © 2019 Cedar Fort, Inc.
Edited by Nicole Terry

Printed in the United States of America

10 9 8 7 6 5 4 3 2 1

Printed on acid-free paper

Contents

CHAPTER 1

When It's Hard

I HAVE SPOKEN AT UTAH STATE PRISON four times now (twice on the men's side, twice on the women's), and it's still probably one of my favorite places I've spoken at. When I got a call to go back and speak for the fifth time, I was elated!

Utah State Prison has Sunday church services as well as something during the week. It was among those services that I would go and speak. But this time would be different because it wasn't church services that reached out to me. This time it was for a drug addiction program graduation. I was told that not only could I not speak on my religion, but I couldn't even mention God at all. I didn't know if I knew how to speak without talking about God, so when they told me that, I was incredibly confused about why they would even think of me to speak to begin with. I tried to think what I would even talk about if I did accept the invitation since I felt I was the most irrelevant speaker they could have chosen. I know nothing about drug addiction or rehab or anything of that nature. I ended up agreeing, and I spoke on change.

I was in their gym and I sat on this makeshift stage they had just for this ceremony. There were hundreds of inmates sitting in front of me all in their matching uniforms. This graduation was a big deal—it was hard to get accepted into the program and it was a lot of work to

1

complete it. For the ceremony it was permitted that family members could attend. But I'll never forget the feeling I had when I saw that very few family members came. I spoke on the reality of change, and that went well and I felt good about the things I shared. I'm not sure if you know this or not, but most, if not all, prisons don't have choirs. But for this graduation ceremony they had a one-time choir sing a song at the closing of it. It was a small group of maybe 15 men that got up, all different ages, some younger than I was and some in their 70's. Some of them were missing teeth, some of them were just the biggest built men that would tower over me, and close to all of them had tattoos all over their faces and their heads. Being a New Yorker, I've seen a whole lot of everything, so it is difficult to be surprised or shocked by anyone, but the men that got up were intimidating men to look at. Now, mind you, this graduation was definitely not a church thing, and definitely not a God thing—it was a drug thing inmates in the prison had to qualify for—but this one-time choir of inmates got up to sing, and I was completely shocked at their choice of song, "A Child's Prayer." I saw these men with their missing teeth and the tattoos on their faces and heads sing and ask, "Heavenly Father, *are you really there?*"

I sat on their makeshift stage and I lost it. The Spirit overwhelmed me in an indescribable way—more than I have ever felt before in my entire life. Because I *felt* so physically that He really was there. That God was very aware of them in that moment and always. That regardless of where they were and what they had done, they were not alone. And I felt so powerfully that they never have been. And neither are we.

But we have these times in our lives when we ask that same question. There are some times we can't help but wonder where He is and if He really is aware of us and if He actually cares and if He even exists at all.

It is well known the raging storm on the water that caused the original Apostles to yell, "Carest thou not that we perish?"[1] But perhaps we can more see ourselves in our personal storms and our heavy thoughts and passing doubts and our pleadings of "Carest Thou not that I'm struggling?! Carest Thou not that this is *so* hard? That this was unwanted?

---

1. Mark 4:38.

That I don't deserve this? That this has been going on for *too* long? Carest Thou not . . . that I don't think I can go on? Carest Thou not . . . about *me*?"

Like the Apostles waking up Christ, who was sleeping during what seemed to be a life-threatening storm, we too sometimes find ourselves wondering if He is sleeping through the times when we feel we so desperately need Him the most. We wonder where relief is, we plead for Him to calm our storm because it's as though we may not make it. Or at the very least, we plead for to Him to wake up—to be conscious, to be mindful, to be present—for our raging storms we're in the midst of.

I have been in too many raging storms, wondering too many times if I will be able to make it, losing my voice too many times because of how loud my pleadings have been, physically aching from wondering if He is sleeping, asking that same question: *Heavenly Father, are you really there?*

Before Lehi had been brought to a large and spacious field where he saw and partook of the fruit, and before he saw the iron rod and the big and spacious building, the very first place he was brought to was a "dark and dreary waste."[2] *Why?* Why was he told to follow a divine being only to be brought right into a dark and dreary place that he was left wandering in for many hours?

What about when Nephi and his family were asked by the Lord to travel years and years in the wilderness to the land of promise, an ongoing trial that threatened his life several times, only to hear the Lord tell them, when they eventually got there and started to settle in, that they needed to leave? To pack up, to keep going, to continue to sacrifice and travel past the promised original counsel and find a different home, the land of Nephi.

What about Alma and Amulek, when they were watching women and children of believers burned for their beliefs and they were restrained by the Lord to stop it? What about in Ether when they

---

2. 1 Nephi 8:7.

traveled in barges for what was much longer than anticipated, and they were buried in the depths of the sea with great and terrible tempests? It was the Lord God who caused that there should be the furious winds and storms on the water.

What about arguably Christ's closest friend, Lazarus, and his two sisters, Martha and Mary? When Lazarus was sick, Christ didn't come to visit. When he died, Christ didn't show up for several days. Where was He then as a close friend? Where was Christ then as someone who is full of miracles? What of the time Joseph Smith was in Liberty Jail while the Saints were suffering? The Prophet of the Lord was pleading for things to be over and things to be different, but months had passed, and he was still in jail.

What about when I joined the Church and I lost all of my friends and had years of silence from family members? What of my and my husband's years of being unemployed while pregnant? What of me following God, who took me away from my home and my family and brought me all the way across the country, just for things to fall apart when I got there? What about all the times I've lost my voice in my prayers because things were getting harder? What about all the times I've prayed and He never answered? Or the countless times I was brought down unwanted and uncharted paths? I, like Lehi, have also been led into dark and dreary places. I, like Nephi, have also been asked to sacrifice *even more*, just when I was confident I couldn't any longer. Like Alma, Amulek, and Joseph Smith, I have also asked for righteous things that were not fulfilled, and *wow* what pain that brought me. Like Lazarus's sisters, Martha and Mary, I have often found myself wondering where Christ is. Wondering why He hasn't come yet, that if He were truly here with me, then my situation could have been avoided. I wonder, like Martha and Mary, if He really does care about me like I thought He did, because relief and miracles have not come yet.

This isn't what I wanted. I didn't ask for this. Why was I led to a dark and dreary place? Where is God in this? How could He let this happen? Why didn't He prevent it? Is God always good? Can He be trusted? Why is it taking so long? Does He really care about me? Is He even there at all? Why do I feel alone? Where are my answers? Where are my promised blessings?

I can think of too many experiences that have caused me to ask these questions, but one that stands out to me was the time I was engaged to a boy that I didn't end up marrying. We had a date set in the temple and everything. He broke it off. He told me that he usually dates "really skinny brunettes" and that he "knew he could find someone much better." Brutal, right? In his defense, he was a really nice man who didn't realize he was being mean but felt that he owed it to me to be honest and thought he was doing the best thing by saying it that way—haha.

But *man*, I had never been crushed so low in my entire life. Reasonably so, right? My self-esteem completely shattered. Even that is an understatement. I left thinking, *I'm not skinny enough, pretty enough, good enough, and bluntly put, I am easily replaceable.* How do you come back from hearing that from someone you were about to marry? How did we even get as far as we did?

But that wasn't the hardest part. Most of all, I had never been more confused in my entire life. This is one of the trickiest things I've gone through, *not* because I wasn't with this guy, but because I thought I was following the Spirit, so how could it not work out? What did I do wrong? Why am I being denied a righteous desire? What's wrong with me? I all of a sudden doubted my relationship with the Spirit—did I even really know Him? Was I doing it wrong the whole time? Every day, no matter how hard I tried to be positive and strong, I'd still break down. I had never been more *spiritually* confused in my life.

Every day I'd find myself screaming and pleading to God that this whole thing would be over and pleading for answers and clarity. I just couldn't make sense of feeling prompted to do something that was going to fail. Yet it seemed it wasn't letting up. I worked overtime every day, doing everything I could to try and get out of this spiritual and emotional slump that I couldn't seem to get out of no matter how many prayers I said. I longed for it to pass, and it didn't. I was mad, thinking that my faith and my God were failing me.

But as I reflected yet again on my lack of progress, I had a new thought. *What if it wasn't God that was failing me. What if it was me?* What if I was improperly placing blame? What if I had it all backward? What if there was a different way to look at all this? What if there were different questions I should be asking? *What good am I overlooking?*

Through my wrestle and my experimenting due to my desperation, I had learned so many more adjectives of the Spirit and of God. What I had known and learned about Them thus far was actually limiting me from allowing Them to show me *what else.* I had unconsciously put a box around Them and what They were capable of doing and how things were "supposed" to be, that I was accidentally dismissing myself from experiencing and recognizing Their vastness of blessings and miracles. I figured if God brings us to something that it should "work out," or if we experience answers to prayers in certain ways that we assume those are the only ways: "I know how to get answers to my prayers, and they come in *this* box because every answer He's given me so far has come *this* way." So when we don't notice it in *that way,* wonder and doubt could take over. But what if He was answering me outside of that box that *I* ignorantly put there to begin with? When I tried to take away these limits that I unconsciously put on Them, I was learning and noticing different ways They were showing me They *were* there and They *were* answering me and trying to guide me and teach me and bring me to better things, and it had just gone over my head.

I roll my eyes thinking about all the time I spent wondering why it didn't work out and where God was in all of this because I failed to see that I was supposed to get engaged all along, that God and the Spirit and my efforts did not fail me. I was supposed to get engaged, but I was not supposed to get married. It was supposed to "not work out" the whole time. It "not working out" was actually it working out perfectly how God had in mind the whole time! Because it led me to a wrestle, which led me to learning vital lessons I couldn't imagine living life without—lessons I would be lost without knowing. Because it all led me to *knowing* God. And when He becomes a reality to you, could you trade that knowledge?

Every bit of pain, confusion, discomfort, and loneliness wasn't for nothing; it was all for the best and 1,000 percent worth it. As hard as things were and continue to be, I know God. And I love Him with a real love.

So whatever it is that we are going through now, what if we ask ourselves, have we got it all backward? Am I improperly placing blame? Am I limiting my God? What if there's another way to look at all this? What if there are better questions to be asking? What if God has something else in mind? What if He knows something we don't? Something greater?

It's sobering to think of Christ, who also asked questions during trials so hard that they caused Him to bleed from every pore, circumstances so brutal that they cost Him His life. I think of when He asked the question to His disciples, "Could ye not watch with me *one hour?*"[3] A parallel question they themselves were asking Him during the raging storm on the sea, "*Could you not be here with me?* Could you have at least been with me as I struggled?" Or during Christ's most painful sacrifice, which caused Him to also wonder and question if He had been forsaken by God Himself. And as Heavenly Father watched His Only Begotten Son be mocked and spit on and falsely judged and murdered, "It pleased the Lord to bruise him."[4] *Why?* Because there was, in fact, something greater to come from it.

I once went to bed on a Saturday trying to think of an excuse so I wouldn't have to go to church the next day. Ever get like that? Where you know it's important to pray and to read, but it doesn't take away from feeling that you just . . . don't want to? I told that to God as I fell asleep. The next morning, it was just Gracie and I at church while Ben stayed home with our sick two-year-old. I woke up surprisingly anxious to take the sacrament. As it was being passed and as I sat there

---

3. Mark 26:40; emphasis added.
4. Isaiah 53:10.

with my eyes closed thinking about the weight of my current situation, my four-year-old daughter grabbed my hand and held it the whole time. There were two convert confirmations and a musical number. This woman sang "All is Well," and it got me thinking.

I don't think "all is well" is referring to times when everything is going smoothly and our lives are free from trials. Perhaps it is referring to times when our soul is content and we feel at peace even among our struggles. Because despite my shortcomings I was so aware of and dealing with even that exact morning, I felt that all was actually well because I felt that God was there with me and loving me and helping me and forgiving me. Even in the middle of an unresolved circumstance, I felt that God was not sleeping.

And I think that's what I love most about the gospel. Not that it prevents us from the blows of life, but that we can feel peace and contentment and love right in the middle of it. Regardless of my shortcomings, regardless of my questions and wondering about His path for me, regardless of my hard times, I felt the Spirit so strongly, and I was so grateful I pushed myself to do what I needed to do most and exercise my power over the adversary.

For three entire days and three entire nights, nonstop, Alma was in the *most bitter* pain. Torment. No breaks. No let-ups. Just paralyzing anguish that kept him crying to God. Completely consuming that whole time. But then, after the longest passing time of immobilizing struggle, he found peace to his soul. And so sometimes we feel like things are *the most* consuming and *the worst* anguish, and we agonize over the passing time with no breaks or let ups, and we have to make the decision to plow through with God and see it through, or we accept and give up.

I know we have these phases where we really have to push ourselves to keep going even when we don't really want to or when we feel like we can't much longer. And I know the weight that comes from not knowing how or when things will work out. But like the three long days and nights in Alma 38, or the 344 days in Ether 6—or perhaps for us in some situations, even longer—as we continue to turn and cry to Christ, He will send angels like He did in Alma, and He will send light like He did in Ether, and we will find peace and forgiveness and strength and change and rest and a new start. Where we don't find an ending to a trial quite yet, we find ease and added strength.[5] Where we can't find answers to prayers quite yet, we find comfort and re-assurance. Where we don't see promised blessings quite yet, we find love and help and continued guidance. We will always find a chance to change and be forgiven. And *oh what a feeling* it is when we see these phases through and realize that the best things can only come from sticking with God at all times and in all things.

Like I felt when speaking in prison, regardless of where we are and whatever we have done and whatever season we may be in, we are not alone. We *will* find peace to our soul. Everlasting struggle just isn't in God's cards. Because really, like Alma said, "There is no other way."[6]

I know how easy it is to wonder and to doubt, but I also know how easy it is for the adversary to skew our perspective when we are trying to make sense of things. He'll get in our vision to stop us from progressing, stop us from doing what is right, stop us from trying, from turning to Christ, and to keep us standing still. I think of Adam and Eve when they were in the garden. The adversary got both of them to hide from the only ones that could help them: Heavenly Father and Christ. Anything that is trying to stop us from trying, to turn around, to give up, to stop crying unto Him, to jump ship—anything to pull us away from God is clear who it is coming from. Holding on to the pattern and promise God set for us that greater things are coming, when He said, "It pleased the Lord to bruise Him," we can move forward knowing there is a better way to understanding. A better way to progress and growth. A better way to the better things.

Are we being productive in our hard times? Are we looking and noticing the good? Are we open to new opportunities? Are we listening? Are we paying attention to our recurring thoughts? Are we standing still? Have we allowed the adversary to run rogue with our thoughts for too long?

---

5. Mosiah 24:15.
6. Alma 38:9.

AL CARRAWAY

What if it's not always about proving ourselves or building our character—what if He is trying to help us discover *His* character? Are we allowing God to be God? Are we giving Him the opportunity to show us how great He really is? What if letting go will allow us to take hold of blessings greater than what we picked out for ourselves? What will happen if we let go of our desire to be in control? What will our life look like if we trust God with our whole heart? What if all of this is not meant to push us away from God, but bring us closer? "Know ye not that ye are in the hands of God? Know ye not that he hath all power?"[7]

Hard will always be there—that won't change. I still wonder and I am still being brought to trials that seem to get harder with time, and I still have to battle the adversary while in the season of making sense of it all. Hard times will always be there, but so will Christ. And with Christ do we overcome and conquer absolutely everything. And with God, we will be brought to the better things—blessings and opportunities and knowledge we wouldn't trade.

Never let a change of course take away from the unchangeable truth that God is taking care of you. Never let our own visions and desires block the unchangeable truth that God knows something we don't. We may not have gone where we had in mind, but we will end up where we need to be, with better blessings, if we but change our perspective and allow things to unfold and blossom in the discomfort and the unexpected and the unwanted and the longer than anticipated. If we but look at things a little differently.

With the reality of our trials come the reality of Christ and the reality of His power, His love, and His purpose to help us succeed. And when we remember all that we have and all that we have been given, when we remember who He really is, then we really can continue through raging waters, knowing He is quite literally with us. And we can continue down uncharted and unwanted paths, knowing He is awake, aware, and actively bringing us to the best things. And we can continue without panic, knowing we are in His hands.

7. Mormon 5:23.

10

And when we plead and wonder, He will lovingly correct us "of little faith, wherefore didst thou doubt?"[8] Because He's never left. He really does care, we really will make it, and it will be *indescribable*. They will *never* give up on us, so let's not give up on Them.

---

8. Matthew 14:31.

CHAPTER 2

When We Doubt

I LISTENED TO THE MISSIONARIES because I felt bad for them and I wanted to prove them wrong. After a few weeks into meeting with them every day, I vividly remember coming home from work late into the night, late enough that the nightlife was already settling down around my apartment and it was becoming a strange kind of quiet. And I remember I was just standing there, looking up at the sky, and I remember thinking: *Is there more than just this? Is there more to me? Are there really answers to the most gut-wrenching questions of the soul? Are there really solid answers to the biggest questions of the universe? Those questions of the soul some people go their whole life looking for and never finding?*

I remember life extremely well not knowing the answers I now. I remember the unrest that came from not knowing, this pit that was in my stomach every time I started to wonder the meaning, if there was one, of why we are here. And I remember extremely well the sweaty palms I got just by driving by a cemetery because of the lack of answers I had about what was going to happen to me. Those feelings are common in the world. But then—

Alma 40:11–12: "The spirits of all men, as soon as they are departed from this mortal body, yea, the spirits of all men, whether they be good or evil, are taken home to that God who gave them life. And then shall it come to pass, that the spirits of those who are righteous are received into a state of happiness, which is called paradise, a state of rest, a state of peace, where they shall rest from all their troubles and from all care, and sorrow."

This is the very first scripture I read in the Book of Mormon. I purposely looked it up when I was learning about the Church. Because to me, if I knew that there really was an answer to the biggest question of the universe, I needed to know what it was. And just like that, I had it. Just in the fifteen seconds it takes to read it, I knew exactly what happens when we die.

As I kept reading, answers to big things just casually came up.

D&C 135:4: "When Joseph went to Carthage to deliver himself up to the pretended requirements of the law, two or three days previous to his assassination, he said: 'I am going like a lamb to the slaughter; but I am calm as a summer's morning.'"

Then I watched the *Joseph Smith: Prophet of the Restoration* movie at the visitors' center, seeing the looks exchanged between Joseph Smith and Emma as he left on a horse, both of them knowing that he was not coming back. And then I watched as the mob came, while bullets were flying everywhere and as the camera panned to the window shattering from the guns, and I heard Joseph say his last words, "*O Lord my God*,"⁹ as he fell to his death. It was then that I felt and *knew* he really was a prophet. Which meant this Church was worth pursuing and learning more about. And then—

Alma 36:15–20: "Oh, thought I, that I could be banished and become extinct both soul and body, that I might not be brought to stand in the presence of my God, to be judged of my deeds. And now, for three days and for three nights was I racked, even with the pains of a damned soul. And it came to pass that as I was thus racked with torment, while I was harrowed up by the memory of my many sins, behold, *I remembered also to have heard my father prophesy unto the people concerning the*

---

9. D&C 135:1.

coming of one Jesus Christ, [emphasis added], a Son of God, to atone for the sins of the world. Now, as my mind caught hold upon this thought, I cried within my heart: O Jesus, thou Son of God, have mercy on me, who am in the gall of bitterness, and am encircled about by the everlasting chains of death. And now, behold, when I thought this, I could remember my pains no more; yea, I was harrowed up by the memory of my sins no more. And oh, what joy, and what marvelous light I did behold; yea, my soul was filled with joy as exceeding as was my pain!"

"The coming of one Jesus Christ?" *Whoa,* that would mean all of that happened and Christ wasn't even born yet. It was reading that scripture that I knew the entire plan of salvation was real. I knew that if Christ could heal and forgive Alma before Christ even came to earth, that meant Christ was preordained to be Christ. That meant that pre-earth really existed. And that meant I existed before I came to this earth. That would mean God was real and I was His. Which meant why I am here has meaning and purpose. And me being here has direction and help and counsel and guidelines.

And that would mean I had the answers to the questions of the universe. Because it was by reading this that I knew where I was to go next after this life was true. And that eternity was a reality.

It was back in 2013 that I was baptized. It was a lot of work to bring me to that decision. It was a lot of work to gain a testimony. It took a lot of studying every day. A ton of prayers throughout the day. It took a lot of acting. A lot of trying. A lot of fasting. A lot of guessing. A lot of unsurety. A lot of experimenting. A lot of focus. A lot of crying. A lot of change. Really hard, completely torn-down and rebuilt kind of change. But to see what comes in return, even all that seems so . . . small.

There was still so much about the gospel I didn't know when I got baptized. But the things that I did know and feel I couldn't push aside. I couldn't feel what I felt and not do anything about it. I got the gift of the Holy Ghost, and I *physically* and immediately felt the contrast and difference. I felt sure. And I felt unstoppable. And I knew nothing would change me from the path I was now on.

And then I moved across the country, following a prompting, and oh man did my heart break. Putting my other really hard trials aside, in my ignorance of being freshly introduced to this gospel, the thought really had never crossed my mind that there were people who had the gospel and didn't do anything about it. I was literally and completely blindsided by something that appeared to be common. I was so sure of this church that I willingly gave up my family so that I could be part of it. I sacrificed my relationship with my dad. I gave up my life to move into the unknown. I gave up and lost everything. Willingly. Because it was true. I had felt much too much and changed much too much to ever question that. And then I saw people not care about it. And my jaw and my heart dropped.

What do you mean there are people who have the Book of Mormon and don't read it? That thing saves lives! What do you mean people don't talk to God every day? We can talk directly to the most powerful, all-knowing being to ever exist, and people just . . . don't? What do you mean people don't know about *this* or about *that* when it's written in our manuals right in front of us?

All those nights I spent looking up into the stars wondering the deepest unanswered questions of the universe that some spend their whole lives seeking after and still not finding. And there are people who have these answers to the deep life mysteries of the world, and they aren't even batting an eye toward it? I couldn't wrap my mind around it.

Looking back to see what we've accomplished and overcome can give us a sense of strength and a reminder of what we're capable of. Looking back can give us a glimpse of making it through things we truly didn't think we could. But sometimes when I would look back at all I overcame and conquered, sometimes I'd ignorantly think, *If I can get through that, I can get through anything.*

Then let's fast forward a little while—

Recently I was vacuuming my living room. And as I was vacuuming, I realized I had just spent a good five minutes entertaining the questions, *What if this isn't true? What if this is all in our heads? What if we made ourselves believe this because it sounds nice? What if all my efforts within the gospel don't matter and I really can live however I want? What if there's not really any way to know what comes next? What if all of this is for nothing?*

And I'd be lying if I didn't admit that those random doubts have come more than that one time. Sometimes they come from trials. Sometimes from idleness. And sometimes just randomly while cleaning the house.

It's interesting, living in the time that we do. Who knew how easy it would be to be influenced by the confusion and the hurt of the world? How dictating the worldly trends could be with our time? Who knew how damaging the distractions of good things are to keep us from the best things? Who knew just how easy it would be to over-complicate enduring? Who knew the subtleties of the adversary could be so damaging, and yet so hard to pick up on sometimes? Who knew how easy it would be to get distracted? How easy it is to lose focus. How easy it is to lose sight of those simple truths of the gospel. How easy it is to second-guess. How easy it is to let passing time dim our promises and blessings.

I know I have found myself asking if this is worth it. Mixed priorities that leave our soul feeling unsatisfied. Passing time where we have nothing to show for our efforts yet. Ongoing trials that have us stretched too thin. Answers that haven't come yet. Promised blessings that haven't been fulfilled yet. How much longer will I stand this? *Is it worth it?*

With all the many trials that come to mind where I question and I doubt and I wonder, I think of the time when I accidentally over-booked my week to travel and speak. During this time, I am living in upstate New York, and accessibility to fly anywhere is limited and exhausting. I can be gone three days only to have spoken one time at one conference for one hour because I would need two whole travel days to get me there and back with layovers and small airplanes going to small airports. I've been public speaking for a long time to where I feel confident and comfortable in the schedule I plan for myself to feel balanced, but moving to the east coast really forced me to dig deep and do some soul searching on my current calling in life. Moving back to where I'm from in New York, after eight years of being in the west coast, was God's idea. But regardless of God being behind it, we hadn't found employment out there. And I don't charge to speak. Sure, a ward member or whoever will use their flier miles to fly me out and back, and my lodging would be covered, but then I would be gone two to three weekends a month, and I would have twelve-plus-hour travel days *one way* of very expensive airport food and Ubers. It added up very quickly. Every time I bought a premade salad only the size of my fist for fourteen dollars at the airport, I would worry about having to pay more later for dinner at my next layover. Each stop in different cities would be a painful reminder of the financial dry season we were in. Eating caused me to question if telling people about God was worth it.

But this one time in particular, when I accidentally overbooked two events in the same week, both were coast to coast. I went coast to coast four times on a total of ten airplanes in six days. I would never do that to myself, but it was an accident and flights were already booked. In between events, I had only a half a day home. After four days traveling to and from Vegas, I was home long enough to eat dinner and tuck my kids in bed before having to go back to the airport to fly to California before the sun even came up. I told my oldest, Gracie, who was four at the time, "I won't be here when you wake up. I have to go back to the airport." She cried. She never cries when I leave, but she was lying in bed and she just cried. She squeezed my hand and said, "You can't go! I need you here with me!" My heart ached, and then it broke.

I dragged my feet and my heavy heart to the airport for another twelve-plus hours on multiple planes and in multiple airports. Delayed flights, expensive layover food, a difficult four-hour time difference, and a trip being at the mercy of strangers who have planned out my whole schedule for me. I text my husband, "Is it worth it? Why do I even do this?" Are my sacrifices even being magnified, or do we just tell ourselves that because it sounds nice? Are my sacrifices even noticed at all? Why do I keep going when I know very well how easy it would be to just . . .

stop? How many times I have asked myself this in so many different capacities and situations where I can't help but start to believe that my efforts and my hope and my faith may be in vain. The things that are hard or are going wrong or unplanned can lead to consuming doubts about if it's worth it and if should we keep going.

Two weeks later, I was traveling to Alberta, Canada. I was gone for three days to speak at two conferences. After traveling all day, I went from the airport right to the church, I changed in the bathroom, and I headed straight to the stand to start speaking. As soon as I sat down after speaking, the long travel day and the time difference kicked in immediately, but I still had a meet-and-greet after. An hour speaking and a two-hour meet-and-greet, followed by an hour drive from Cardston to Lethbridge, and I got in at around 1 a.m. New York time. I was so exhausted I just dead-weight face planted on the bed of a really nice rental condo on a golf course in a gated community. I woke up at 4:30 a.m., mostly due to the time difference, and then *I saw it*. A bug. I killed it, no big deal. But then I saw another one. And then another one. And after killing a few just from lying down, I noticed the amount of blood I would see when I mushed them. I knew what that could mean. I flung myself up in bed and lifted up my pillow and saw *lots* of them. I jumped out of bed with my heart pounding and pulled back the covers and saw something I never want to see again. I ran out of the bedroom and stood on kitchen tile floor for over three hours until whoever it was that was my contact for this area—I didn't even remember their name—woke up.

Bed bugs. *Lots of them.* I had seventy-two bites *just* on my neck and face. There were bites on my ears, eyelids, both of my arms, and palms of my hands, and every one of my fingers was completely covered. A bad reaction from the bites spread across my stomach in a rash, my legs were gross, and the bites on my feet turned into gashes from the severe itch that felt like constant burns. An itch and a pain that is indescribably terrible, I wouldn't wish it upon the vilest of person. I still had to speak that night, and in my hand while I was speaking was Cortisone cream that I would put on my hands and arms while speaking at the pulpit because of how constant the itch and pain was. I looked like I had chicken pox . . . or leprosy. I ended up having to throw out most of my belongings as well has having to take a trip to urgent care. I was pregnant with my third at the time, so I couldn't be put on a steroid they said I desperately needed, and because of that, healing was going to be slow. Scabs were all over my face and my whole body. It took two weeks just for my makeup to try and cover it up. I still have so many scars from this ordeal. Now you can imagine I'm having those same thoughts as two weeks previous, right? *Why?! Is this worth it? If God were real, then why would He let this happen? I am doing something for Him. Where are my blessings?! Maybe there are no blessings and this is all in my head?*

I walked up and sat on the stand before those devotionals began in both California and in Canada and looked out on a thousand youth. And then, it happened. My reason. My purpose. *God.* All of a sudden, looking out and seeing everyone I felt just a sliver of how God sees them, and *wow* was it electrifying! I watched them cry tears that needed to be cried. Some laughed some long-overdue laughs. I watched some step foot into a church for the first time in a long time. I connected with many who had no words to speak, just a tight grasped hug. I saw chains broken, promises made, weight lifted, determination renewed, revelation received, hope refilled, and souls strengthened, all because of the power of the Spirit and the reality of Christ. Those few-hour-long meet-and-greets I had after, I was hugging and listening and feeling, being shown person by person just how personal and individual God really is to each of us. I was reminded exactly of what God wanted from me, and I was reminded overwhelmingly that He is always worth the effort and He and this church are worth sacrificing for.

I look back on all the trials I have been through since joining the Church. I'd never known loneliness until I got baptized. I'd never known such painful sacrifice and loss until I joined the Church. I'd never known real pain until then. Indescribable anguish. I'd never struggled so long and so hard where my body would literally ache before, until I got baptized. When I got baptized and decided to follow God, for a while it seemed as though things were falling apart. Times when I felt my desperate pleadings weren't heard, or I was asked to do something so painfully hard. I talk openly about me screaming at God until literally losing my voice, wondering where He was, if He even cared still about *me*, or if He was even there at all.

It would be *too easy* to blame all of this on God. It would be too easy to step back and realize this would never have happened if I didn't put forth the effort. None of those things happened until I tried to turn to this "supposed God" and turn back where things made sense and where things were comfortable, back to where twenty-one years of habit, tradition, contentment, and culture lay deep within my roots.

Like you, I also know what it's like to feel like you have nothing to show for your efforts. Like you, I also know what it is to wonder, to doubt, to struggle, to sink, to feel judged, abandoned, unwanted, unworthy, tried, tired, and alone. Like you, I know how hard it is to keep going sometimes. Where we feel as if we are hanging on by our fingertips when we are being pulled by our ankles in the opposite direction. Losing our voice, losing hope, losing strength. Forcing ourselves to use faith we don't even know if we have or not. But I also know how worth it and possible it is to keep going and see it through.

It's productive to evaluate those questions and wonders we have. It's also productive to evaluate first our efforts. We often are quick to blame others and blame God and our situation for lack of progress, but sometimes when I take an honest step back, I will see that I have not been doing my part. I fall into the category of those who "did not look unto the Lord as they ought."[10] I have not been taking advantage of the simple things of the gospel. I have looked over those things we have been taught first on what we should be doing daily. I have to remember that I can't just expect everything to come into my lap when I myself am not investing the appropriate time into seeking and listening and turning to Him. And not just seeking and listening and looking for what *I want*. Where are your efforts? Can improvements be made? Do we need to change? Are we investing the time? The adversary is subtle, and his craft is to make us think those things aren't important or are irrelevant or not a priority or too simple.

---

10. 1 Nephi 15:3.

But how can we expect answers when we aren't turning to God? How can our doubts get taken care of when we don't do anything about them? How can He answer us when we do not speak to Him? When we do not ask Him? When we don't read His words and counsel in the scriptures? How can we expect anything to help us when we aren't doing what we can to receive that help? How can we think the gospel isn't for us if we aren't learning about it and actively living it? How can we make that decision if we don't actually know what it really is? We can't.

I was on a Skype chat once with two missionaries and a man who was learning about the Church. After the lesson, the man thanked us for the lesson but said he really only came to tell the missionaries that this church was not for him. He didn't find the answers he was looking for. As we were about to sign off, I asked what he thought of the scriptures the elders asked him to read from his lesson previous. After he admitted that he never read them, he confessed to never reading the Book of Mormon at all on his own, just the few verses the missionaries would sometimes share during a lesson. I asked him if he asked his questions in prayer, and when he had said no, I smiled a subtle smile, having seen the disconnect.

Are we actively doing something about our questions or doubts, or are we letting them linger and hold us back? Are we remembering and doing the simple things of the gospel? Whatever we do, not doing anything is making things worse. No one can do it for us except us. It is through those simple things we have been taught first, whether in Primary or by missionaries, where we can productively move forward working through and growing and learning and moving onward and upward. Why are we taught them first? Because the power that we are told that comes from doing those things is not wishful thinking, it's real. Just like the time I took when investigating, answers and progress came even with my deep *lack* of knowledge and understanding and experience because I invested the effort and simply tried. Am I still trying and investing as much as I did back then?

Another thing to consider during a situational season of doubting—doubting if we can make it, doubting if things will get better, doubting that promised blessings are coming, doubting God's will or timeline or His path for us: *Are we allowing God to be God?* Are we allowing ourselves the opportunity for God to show us how great He really is? Are we pushing through to see it to the end? Are we accepting the passing time to give God the chance to give us these experiences where we are reminded of our reason and our purpose and we just *feel* this electrifying moment that reminds us of why we are here and what we need to be working toward?

Sometimes I'll read old journal entries about my trials and confusion, and I look back at all these nights I spent collapsed on the floor, screaming at God until I'd lose my voice, "*I can't do this!* This is too hard, I'm not this strong!"—those times when I asked where He was or why nothing was coming together yet—those moments when I was brought down to desperately low levels of anguish that I had never before felt. And sometimes I'll see old pictures of myself and think of how I had no idea how my life would unfold. No idea what lay ahead or where God would bring me next. And to see what I have now and what I'm doing, I can't help but smile.

I wish I could just yell to myself in the past, "*YOU'LL BE ALL RIGHT! YOUR LIFE TURNS OUT AWESOME!*" But of course it turns out awesome, because that's what God will always do for us. We may not be free from trials and challenges, and we may not have all the answers we want about our future, but we know enough: we are led by an all-powerful, all-loving God. And if having the most powerful Being to ever exist on our side isn't empowering, then I don't know what is.

So when we truly know and remember all that, even during our struggles, we can smile. And we can laugh. And we can wipe off our mascara and move on. And we can keep going. And we can live a better life. And we can enjoy the unexpected.

Yeah, maybe we have these moments in our life that slow us down and bring more doubt and discouragement than hope and excitement. But these sometimes-heavy doubts don't take away from the truthfulness of the gospel. And these doubts, whether fleeting or lingering, cannot take away from what I felt when I stood in the Sacred Grove saying my first prayer ever with the missionaries. Those doubts from the adversary, no matter how crafty, cannot take away from what I felt when I did temple work for all four of my grandparents. And my aunt. And my uncle. *Goose bumps.* Nothing can take away from what I felt at not just those firesides in California and Canada but every single fireside I have ever spoken at. Or that moment yesterday, driving home in silence from the store with my windows down, when I heard as clear as day to just *hold on a little longer,* and I just *felt* so overwhelmingly that there is no way this gospel is not true and that this work is not true and God is not true and what we're working toward is not true. It's impossible.

Elder Ballard said, "I encourage you to stop and think carefully before giving up whatever it was that brought you to your testimony of the restored Church of Jesus Christ in the first place. Stop and think about what you have felt here and why you felt it. Think about the times when the Holy Ghost has borne witness to you of eternal truth."[11]

Can you think of a time when you felt the Spirit? Can you think of a time when you felt hope? Peace? Love, forgiveness, happiness, laughter, comfort? Because all things that are good are God showing Himself to us. All good things are because of Christ. I hope that every day we take time to notice Him because He is always here, and we feel Him every day more than we recognize.

So yeah, maybe we do that all-too-familiar dance with the adversary, but then we have these moments in our life...where we feel and experience . . . *so deeply* . . . that we have no words to describe exactly what happened or how we felt . . . but we just know that *electrifying* feeling is from God and from this gospel, a feeling that trumps all feelings of doubt or discouragement. No doubt can hold up against those feelings.

No pathetic attempt from the adversary can take away from the reality of those times we have felt the Spirit. Where we have felt *Him.*

---

11. "To Whom Shall We Go?" *Ensign,* Nov. 2016.

Sometimes the feelings are not as often as we'd hope, but passing time and the adversary cannot take away from the reality of the times when we have our heart beat just a little bit faster. When we have felt goose bumps. When we have felt renewed hope, renewed strength to face an unchanging situation. When we have felt our eyes fill and we know if we blink a tear will fall, so we try so hard not to blink. Or those times when we hear a small voice saying to just hold on a little longer. Or we feel our soul jolt and dance within us. And I can't deny that every time I have felt those electrifying feelings, I was living the gospel. And I was seeking after Him. Because I sure as heck never felt those goosebump moments that set my soul dancing *before* I got baptized.

I'm really grateful for those sometime rare feelings to help me stay focused on why we're here and what we need to be doing. I'm grateful I have taken the time to *write them down,* so in the future when I don't feel it when I need it most, when I allow doubts to creep in longer than I should, I am reminded of those undeniable times that I in reality *feel Him* through His spirit to bring me back.

Do we realize what we're a part of? Do we realize this is actually real? Do we realize and remember the power we have? Do we realize and remember that what we do now affects our forever? And are we living in a way that aligns with that? Are we treating it as we should? And if we don't know yet, are we doing something about it?

Yeah it takes work, but all things do. The trick to losing weight? Work. The trick to getting good grades? Work. The trick to getting a real testimony? Work. The trick to keeping a testimony? Work. But can we think of anything more important than endless life and eternal bliss?!

Let's make taking care of ourselves and our souls a priority. Make God a priority. This gospel is not our last option; it is our only option. Because this isn't just wishful thinking—it's real. And once we know it, let's do everything we can to hold on to it and stay focused. To love it, we have to live it. We have to give this a real go at it! Every day. We have to continuously choose Him over the fleeting things of this world. We have to stay focused. Because we won't know until we act. We can't know what it can do for us in our lives if we don't let it into our lives. He can't help us if we don't give Him anything to help us with.

Because we are meant for something *so much greater than this*— so much greater than the here and now, greater than the worldly "happiness" that isn't even a sliver of the godly and heavenly that's available to us through the simple principles of the gospel so many so often overlook.

Let's recommit to act. Let's recommit to read. Let's refocus on the principles of the gospel. Let's recommit to study, really study. To learn. To turn to Him. To talk to Him. To preach. To participate. To always exercise our change of heart muscle. And to keep going. Let's recommit to Him. To trusting Him, His commandments, and His path for us. Because every single bit of it is worth the sacrifice, the time, the trust, the loss . . . Because sacrifice, suffering, loss, etc., doesn't even come close to what we receive in return. Because His promises are real. And He will show us. But we have to continuously put in the effort. And if we need a reminder of our blessings, remember D&C 6:22–23, remember that "night that you cried unto me in your heart, that you might know concerning the truth of these things," and that He spoke "peace to your mind concerning the matter? What greater witness can you have than from God?"

And if we need a reminder of our blessings, remember that our hearts are still beating. And remember that we have the answers to the questions of the universe. Remember that we are His, and that is *everything*.

But what of the times when it's out of our hands?

CHAPTER 3

When Trusting God Is Hard

IS GOD ALWAYS GOOD? I think of the extreme faith and sacrifice of Mary as she accepts to be the mother of Christ. I think of the discomfort of her last few days of her pregnancy, the hardest parts in my opinion of pregnancy, and having to ride for days on a donkey. I think of all her pleadings to God she must have had as she had all of these opportunities to rest pass her by. I think of the dirty animal stall they laid in to bring a newborn into the world. Was it because she did something wrong? Was it because God is not always good?

I think of Alma and Amulek, who devoted their lives to serving God. I think of them being restricted by the Spirit to save all of the believers who were being burned to death in front of them. I think of their days of their consistent and relentless persecution and abuse from everyone around them. I think of them imprisoned and of their possible confusion as to why things needed to be this way, why after their efforts to do good they were being punished. Where was God, who allowed them to be in this situation? Why couldn't He have avoided this part for them? Is it because God does not always care?

I think of me. I think of my sacrifices and changes of course and unfulfilled requests and desires, and I wonder, *Who is this God that allows these things to happen?*

Here's how it usually goes for me: when I pray and ask Heavenly Father for things I need or would like help with, it's what I want and see best for myself. It's an unconscious and obvious thing, mostly. If I have a day of travel, I'm going to ask that I'll be safe and my planes won't be delayed or canceled. If I am interviewing for a job, I ask to get it. If I need to wake up early, I pray that my alarm will go off and I don't sleep in. I'm going to assume we all do this to some degree. But what if things we are naturally asking for all the time are stopping us from other things that should be happening? What if those little things aren't God's will? What if there's something *different* and something *better?*

This is a long story for a different time, but in 2016 we were unemployed for seven months and down to our last few hundred dollars in our savings account. *Oh,* I cannot count the job interviews my husband and I had. Pleading for them to be right because we were desperate. And I mean *desperate.* I was pregnant with our second kid with no health insurance and our bank account dwindling. We looked all over Arizona, where we were living. Every day for seven months. We first approached the trial with optimism and faith, but then a month passed. And then another month passed. And then reality seemed to knock out our optimism. I had a paralyzing need to know if my baby was safe and healthy because we hadn't been able to go the doctor yet— *oh* to have just heard a heartbeat. And two months turned into seven months, and trying to support our growing family seemed impossible as our savings account was thinning quickly.

Fear became a physical feeling. We felt as if all our efforts and faith were in vain. Passing time drained our energy and our hope. God was letting us down multiple times, each and every unsuccessful job interview. He was letting us fall and letting this happen. Maybe He even stopped listening to our pleadings. Maybe He didn't care about this. Maybe God is not always good.

I was on my tenth plane due to that accidental double scheduling to speak—from home in New York to Vegas and then back home, then back out to Santa Barbara, California, and then home again. Four coast-to-coast trips in six days, only home for half a day in between. Of course, I prayed for good flights to make it home to be with my kids. But on my third plane on my trip home, I had both a delayed flight *and* a canceled flight. *Why?* What about my faithful prayers? Wasn't this simple enough to bless me with, a smooth journey home as a blessing for my missionary efforts of devotionals I did? God did not seem to care about my fatigue from four full travel days on planes and from the four-hour time difference and from my first-trimester symptoms while pregnant with our third baby. He did not seem care enough about my desperation to make it home to my two kids, who had woken up every morning all week I was gone asking if today was the day I would come home. God did not seem to care about the tears from my four-year old pleading for me to be there.

But what if we got it all wrong? What if there's something else, a something *better* and a something *different*? As someone who is constantly having things go unplanned and unexpected, I know there is.

On my way home, I was exhausted from the time difference of California and New York. I was exhausted of constantly waiting for flights and sitting for too long. I was annoyed from having to pay for four days of meals with expensive airport food while both my husband and I were unemployed. I was nauseous from all this traveling and being first-trimester pregnant. I was finally making it home from six days of what seemed to be too much for my body and my kids to handle. I had three planes to get me back, but one plane was delayed, and then another was canceled. After talking to an agent for a while, I was rerouted, and it pushed back my landing time by six hours. My seat was on the first row, which meant I couldn't have my bag on the ground under the seat in front of me. It would have to go in an above compartment, but the only available space was in the back of the plane. It may seem silly, but in my mind in this current situation, it was just another little something to make things a little worse because it would mean I couldn't easily get my laptop out to write. And writing was the one thing I wanted to do that I felt I had control over.

I sat next to an off-duty pilot who just *loved* to talk. Don't get me wrong—I always go out of my way to talk to strangers at the airport. It's like a sport of mine. But I hadn't slept more than three hours in two days, and after being social to a crowd of eight hundred teenagers, I was too tired to talk and be social. I was burnt out. But this pilot next to me just. kept. going. Through my tired nods to him I just kept thinking in my mind, *Looks like I don't get to write at all. Looks like one more thing that's going against me.* He told me all about his five-year old, who had blonde hair even though he and his wife are brunettes, and he told me all about what schooling to become a pilot was like. He brought up his fear with ISIS and social media, and he talked about how living in Indiana is *just okay.* He asked why I travel so much, and he asked what I talk about as a public speaker after I answered him. "God," I told him, and he told me about how he went to college with "a Mormon" once we got to that part in our conversation.

And then it came. God, with the something different. The something better. Halfway through this flight home in the middle of this unwanted situation, I recognized God in the unexpected and the unplanned and His hand in all these intricate details. I experienced His attention to me and to others because it *didn't* go how I asked.

This man told me about when he was a pilot in the army and his deep, deep fear and unrest with how God saw Him because of it. He literally stuttered to tell me how he doesn't know how he can forgive himself or if what he did while serving was okay. He told me about the weight he has carried for eight years wracked with this unrest. We had an inspired conversation, and the Spirit was so present it jolted my soul within and fatigue was far, far away. I don't know what I said—no credit to myself in the least bit—but it ended with him saying, "This is the clarity I have been tirelessly seeking for so, so many years. This . . . is incredible."

We have unconsciously limited our God to only a handful of adjectives, and by doing so we reject His vastness of profound love and miracles. What if God did hear me and my pleadings? What if He does care about me and my kids? But you know, what if He also cares about this pilot from Indiana and *his* tired pleadings, which were not seven months long, like our unemployment, but *eight years* long? What if all of this, our life and such, is something so much bigger than just us? What if we are unconsciously rejecting ourselves from having an abundance of experiences that leave us feeling *incredible?* Are we *allowing* God to be God? Are we allowing God the opportunity to show us how great He really is?

I am certain that there is something else that God is behind. I am certain God knows something we don't. I am learning the vastness and intricate details of God in *everyone's* lives, not just mine. And what a *thrill* it is to see it unfold.

Surely everything about Christ's birth was according to God's plan. What seemed like unanswered prayers and rejection were just keeping them on a path to fulfilling prophecy. If things were different, would the shepherds have found them? I'm not sure. And thinking of Alma and Amulek, we think that God should protect us from these unwanted or unfair situations that we sometimes don't get to the part where the Lord grants us "power" for a greater miracle.[12] Everyone was slain, all those who were persecuting and abusing them were all killed in the destruction of the prison, *except* Alma and Amulek. They stood *in the midst* of destruction completely safe and spared, and they saw an even bigger miracle than avoidance. Would Alma and Amulek love and know God as well if God made it so prison never happened and they never experienced its destruction and their incredible protection? Would they have experienced this *incredible* miracle that showed them just how powerful and good God really is?

After almost my entire pregnancy not knowing if my baby was healthy, getting down to our last forty dollars in our account, and living completely off someone else's food storage, I saw it. I saw God. Allowing the unexpected and the passing time, we saw the something different and most definitely the something better. We were blessed with a *better* job with *better* pay, an almost threefold financial increase from the job I lost previous, in a *different* state with better health insurance

---

12. See Alma 14:28.

with *better* hospitals, moving into a *better* home more fit for the space we needed for our new addition, in a different church building with callings and friendships that impacted us for our whole lives.

Are we going to complain that we are "captive" or struggling, or are we going to hold out faithful for a bigger miracle?[13] Because it's our unwanted and our hard that allow us to know and understand God better than ever and be brought to the better things.

So then why is trusting God so hard? If it is true that we have the most powerful being to ever exist on our side, then why is it so hard to allow His will to take over? Why is it so hard for us to give it all to Him fully and completely? If it is true that we have an all-knowing God who makes no mistakes and is always on our side, then why is it so hard to let go and live the way He wants us to? Why is it so hard to let Him take care of us? Why wouldn't we want things to go how our perfect God wants them to? Why is it so difficult to fully give it to Him? Why is it so hard to let God be God?

I can think of several things off the top of my head, but it all comes down to one thing for me. It could mean uncharted, unmarked, unwanted paths. It could mean giving up comfort or passions. Because giving it to God means an unexpected outcome. If we give it to Him, what is he going to do with it? An unknown variable brings fear and hesitation, the playground for the adversary.

The adversary usually gets to me more in my thoughts and hypotheticals than anything else. Thoughts that could have the power to immobilize us and stop us from making even a step in the right direction simply because it's on a new, uncharted path for us. Thoughts and doubts that can be so crippling that we become heavy enough for no movement, entertaining all the worst-case scenarios and what ifs. Fear and wonder that can be so powerful that they turned Lot's wife into a pillar of salt. And it wasn't necessarily because she physically looked back that it destroyed her, but because she looked back *longingly.* She entertained those dangerous and immobilizing thoughts from

---

13. See Alma 14:28.

the adversary and started to believe that "nothing that lay ahead could possibly be as good as those moments she was leaving behind."[14] She doubted the Lord's ability to bring her somewhere better.

It wasn't until I got baptized that things started to fall apart in my life for the first time it seemed. I lost just about everyone. I had a new and foreign loneliness with silence from my closest family members. I'd spend any free time with missionaries because it seemed as though they were all I had most times. And wow was I elated when I decided I was going to serve a mission of my own. Elated to tell God my decision, knowing His excitement and approval to do something that is righteous and good. It wasn't just confusion I had when my answer was to move to Utah instead—it was anger. That was not what I wanted, and it was not what I asked for. *Maybe if I asked differently, reworded my prayer, I would get a different answer?* Not the case. And it wasn't just me that was angry, but can you imagine the anger from my family? As if they didn't already think this way before, *this church* was tearing our family apart. And how could I explain it to them? I was going all the way across the country to a place I had never been where I didn't know a single person. And for what? A so-called God? And it wasn't like a mission or school where you have the idea you could maybe one day make it back home; it was for the rest of my life as far as I was concerned at that time. My dad had stopped speaking to me because of my decision to get baptized and now, against my will, I left the only way of living that I knew of, having to cope with the idea I could potentially never see him ever again.

Although I saw this as the biggest trial of my existence, I saw Utah as my glimmer of hope. Things had been so bad since baptism, and I saw this, the place where God Himself was bringing me, as a time for things to come together and start making sense and to become a little easier and better. Unfortunately, when I got there, things had only gotten much worse. I quite literally wrote and published an entire book on the trials that followed from stepping out of the font to a new life in the West. Unanswered prayers and judgments and sacrifice and loneliness and criticizing too overpowering to put into a reader's digest

---

14. Jeffrey R. Holland, "'Remember Lot's Wife': Faith Is for the Future," BYU Speeches, Jan. 13, 2009.

version for you. Here I was thinking things were going to get better, but my uncharted and unwanted and unexpected path I was currently on seemed debilitating and dark. And to make things just a *little* worse, on top of it all, my blankets somehow never made it into my car for the cross-country trek. I would go home to a basement apartment I had by myself and sleep on the floor wrapped in a towel. This is where God's path had brought me.

I have a closeness with Laman and Lemuel. I am Laman and Lemuel, and you know, if we can look past the whole multi-attempted murders of their brother Nephi, I don't think they're that bad—haha. They were told they needed to move and flee into the wilderness because Jerusalem was going to be destroyed. But guess what? After *years* of traveling and wandering and sacrificing and never settling down, guess what was still there? Jerusalem. You have to side with them on this one when they vocalize their fatigue and wonder and even anger.

"He hath led us out of the land of Jerusalem, and we have wandered in the wilderness for these many years; and our women have toiled, being big with child; and they have borne children in the wilderness and *suffered all things, save it were death*; and it would have been better that they had died before they came out of Jerusalem than to have suffered these afflictions. Behold, these many years we have suffered in the wilderness, which time we might have enjoyed our possessions and the land of our inheritance; yea, and *we might have been happy*."[15]

They're mad. They're mad they have to sacrifice and change. They're mad they had to leave their life and their friends and their comfort and to live different than anyone else. And for what? Destruction that hadn't even happened yet?

And so there I was on the floor of my new home in Utah, wrapped in a towel, dealing with what it was that was breaking me, and I couldn't help but wonder, *Why? And for what? Blessings that haven't even happened yet?* With passing time and increased hardships and diminishing strength and lack of answers, I found myself running

---

15. 1 Nephi 17:20–21, emphasis added.

thin on optimism. I found myself, like Lot's wife, failing to see God bringing me somewhere better. How can I trust God if even after all these efforts I haven't seen my something—*anything*—better? How can I trust God is always good when it doesn't seem I have any anything to show for it?

But then I remembered something: *God.* I remembered Who He *really* is and His entire purpose and existence. I remembered Amulek's response to Alma when he asked if they, too, were going to be burned: "Be it according to the will of the Lord."[16] Surely if Amulek can have that kind of faith and trust when he was staring at literal death and flames in front of his eyes, death to captivity, I could also muster enough faith to say, "*So be it.*" Because regardless of passing time, regardless of where we are on a certain path, and regardless of how crafty and powerful the adversary is when we let him into our heads, it cannot take away from the reality that God's entire existence is to lift us higher and make us better. Recognizing that those unwanted, uncharted, and unexpected paths that are really hard are only seasons. And seasons don't last forever.

If I gave up when my dad asked me to choose him or the Church, one of my sisters would not have eventually gotten baptized like she did. If I had never endured the brutal life early on in Utah, I would have never discovered writing and blogging. My two previous books I've done quite literally never would have happened. If I had listened to the adversary and gone back to where things made sense and where things were comfortable, I would have never met my husband. I wouldn't have my kids. I would have never become a public speaker, something that makes me feel my true self. I would have never overcome and learned and grown and gained and become who I am now without those paths and seasons. And I *really like* me. God has brought me to *and through* everything I would never trade for anything.

Quite literally, with no bit of exaggeration, I wouldn't have a *single* thing I have now if it weren't for God and *His* ways. I wouldn't have a single thing I have now if it weren't for every single moment I was wondering where He was and if He really did care about me. Because it

16. Alma 14:13.

was every single time I was wondering where He was that has brought me to *everything* I have now, and it breaks my heart to imagine my life *any* different.

Is God always good? Does He always care? It's all true. And our faith and our efforts are not in vain, if we but see our season through and if we but stay on that unexpected path, allowing ourselves to let God be God. Because just like in the very first chapter on the very first page of 2 Nephi, Jerusalem was destroyed. Promises and prophecies were fulfilled. Because regardless of how tempting and logical the adversary can seem, our promises, too, *will* be fulfilled.

What thoughts are we entertaining in our minds? Are we Alma, wondering *what if?* Or are we Amulek, saying, "So be it"? Are we allowing the adversary to win simply by standing still? Because if there's one thing I know about Satan, it's that he will do anything that simply keeps us from taking even one step closer to what God wants us to be doing. Are we moving? Are we seeing it through and allowing life and its promised blessings to unfold and blossom?

Sometimes we don't always know the *what* or the *why* behind things, but we do always know the who. Embrace the unexpected knowing who is guiding you. A God who is always good. A God who has helped us before, who will help us again. A God who has comforted and saved and guided before, who will do it again. A God who solely exists to bring us to the better and to make us better. And seeing Him through one hard or unexpected time, and seeing the blessings that come from that, will make it easier to trust Him the next time. And then the next. And then you'll find yourself on the ride of your life, a ride you were always intended to take. And then times will come when we will find ourselves feeling at ease even among trials, because from consistently trying to trust, we will have experienced time and time again that we are being led to the greater things. Then times will come when the smiles are real. And the happiness is real. Regardless of our situations. Times will come when the scary and the hard and the unexpected turn into exciting, thrilling new adventures that come with peace, with our knowledge that we are in motion to the best-fit blessings.

And we'll be profoundly grateful things didn't go our own way because we will find ourselves living our best self in our best life, living and experiencing things we didn't even know were available to us, with new knowledge and talents we wouldn't have wanted to go any further in life without. Because we chose to trust the most powerful being to ever exist.

And we will one day pause and look around, and we'll see where we are, what we've gained along the way, the something different and the something much better. And we'll wonder why we hadn't done better all along. Because one day we, like the pilot I sat next to, will come to moments of clarity and lifted weight, and we'll truly feel that "*This . . . is incredible.*" And we wouldn't want to change a thing. So if we give it to God, what's He going to do with it?

Magnify it.

CHAPTER 4

When God Makes Us Wait

ABOUT A MONTH AFTER BAPTISM, back in 2009, I remember telling friends of mine from my singles branch of my answer to move to Utah in response to serving a mission. They said, "Are you sure?" Still learning how the whole Spirit and receiving answers to prayers worked, I responded that I was pretty sure because I couldn't get the idea out of my head. Then they both seemed really puzzled and then asked if I knew what false revelation was. I didn't. They told me about a close married couple of theirs who were expecting their second baby. The husband and wife both had gone to the temple together on a regular monthly temple trip, not seeking any specific revelation out of their service this particular day. The husband and wife went separate ways and met back up in the celestial room. And to their astonishment they both had the same exact impression as each other during their time worshiping apart in the temple. The husband turned to his wife and said, "We're having a boy, and *this* is what we're going to name him." And the wife, completely surprised, said something along the lines of, "No way! I also was told that we are having a boy and that we should name him the same thing!" Is that not the coolest experience?! They both separately received the same exact revelation as each other. It leaves little, if any, room for doubt. Well, guess what? Their second child was born, and it was a girl. And then their third child was born, and it was also a girl.

Wait, what? How did that happen? How did they both have that come to them on their own and then both of them were just . . . wrong? Now, a month into baptism, there was much too much I didn't know or understand, but one thing I thought I knew for certain was that the house of the Lord was where you can go to get away from false thoughts and confusion and have that intimate one-on-one time with God and His spirit. In my early learning and piecing together and experimenting, one thing that I wasn't willing to accept was this idea of false revelation in the context of this experience. But who was I to say? I'm not them. I knew close to nothing at this point of my spiritual journey, and regardless of what I thought I knew, that didn't change the reality of them having three girls. As the years passed and as I grew in understanding, I would think back on this story frequently—I'm not sure why. I just thought the whole thing was bizarre.

Fast forward to 2013, I was sitting in the celestial room with Ben, who was at the time just my fiancé. I had never talked about home and definitely didn't express, or even feel at the time, any desire to ever move back to New York. I had accepted God's will that I was to be in the West, and I had built a new life for me from the dust. I was proud of what I had created and the things I was doing and accomplishing. And Ben looked me right in the eye in the celestial room and said with confidence, "I'm going to bring you home." I knew what he meant, and hearing him say it the way he did made me smile with excitement.

I've written down every single priesthood blessing I have ever gotten since the year I got baptized. I knew exactly what God promised to me specifically and *when* He promised it to me. I know exactly what He's asked of me and things I need to change. I read that journal often; it's my favorite one I keep. I've counted six priesthood blessings total over the years that have mentioned me moving home to New York and the experiences I'll have with my family. *Six.* Two years had passed since the experience in the celestial room with Ben telling me that, and we eventually did end up moving. But to Arizona. And that was right and inspired by God. And then, inspired by the Spirit, the time came for us to move again! And after a few more blessings mentioning New

York, we moved back to Utah. And years had passed in Utah, and that move was profoundly right and guided by God.

So then, what happened? Was Ben just being nice? Was he just talking out of hope and good intentions? What of all the promised blessings I had gotten saying I was to move to New York? Years and years passed, and many moves later—four houses to be exact—NY still never seemed to have been His will for us. I mean, we tried! We did, we really tried. Every time I had gotten a blessing mentioning it throughout the years, we looked into it that same day to make it happen, and every time, it just *didn't*. Opportunities and God's guidance had brought us other ways. So how could God in a priesthood blessing be different from God speaking to us through other ways?

Receiving no counsel to stop us otherwise, we had just signed our lease for another year in Utah, when a month later, *it came back.* The idea of New York. We were in sacrament meeting when someone spoke on patriarchal blessings. Ben and I turned to each other at the same time and we both said, "Let's read ours together again when we get home." So we did. Two hours passed, and it was fine—we were glad we did it—but nothing too big came of it. Until we went to stand up and cook dinner, and yet again Ben looked at me and said, "We gotta go." Now you can imagine I took it with a grain of salt this time, right? But we moved forward with it anyway, yet again. We planned and prepared and looked into, all while I was waiting for God to stop us like all of the countless times He had before. Except this time, He didn't stop us. This time, everything fell into place. We had gotten ahold of a realtor and got approved to buy a house before morning even came. And two weeks later, thanks to FaceTime and the gift of discernment, we bought a house across the country without ever seeing it in person. We closed on our house in twenty-seven days, I quit my job at the Church Office Building, and Ben took one car with our two giant dogs and I took our other car with our two kids, and we drove across the country to our new home within seven minutes of my family. I hate to admit that I was so certain something was going to make our plans fall through again and this whole thing had been a sham that we didn't even tell my family what we were doing! I was so psyched out from false hopes and empty promises that I didn't believe this was actually happening until we pulled into our driveway of our new home in Rochester, New York. It wasn't until then that I thought it was finally safe to tell my family what we were up to. They had no idea! We went to their houses in person and gave them the surprise of their lives!

I left with only my dog and clothes when I first started my journey across the country to Utah, completely by myself, sleeping on the floor, wrapped in a towel (I meant to bring my blankets. I'm not sure what happened). No job. No friends. No idea where I was going or why I was even going. Just my dog and a tiny little testimony just barely getting started, guessing my way around faith with a whole lot of hope that God was as good as He promised He'd be if I trusted Him. I started from scratch. I've achieved and conquered and sacrificed and built and expanded and grown and gained everything I have now from a million little decisions several times a day to continuously choose to trust.

I returned with a husband, two kids, two cars, two one-hundred-pound dogs, an entire moving truck, two published books, a *lot* of experiences, a lot of new talents, a *ton* of conquered trials, an unstoppable passion, and an indescribable amount of gratitude and was welcomed by repaired relationships from the blessing of time and the grace of God. Full circle.

Now you know my years of unrest I've had with this husband and wife temple thing. Here's the honest report back: As everything was coming together for us, you can imagine their experience from 2009 came into my mind again. And here I was in 2018 trying to Facebook stalk a family I'd never met before. There they were. Many, many years and a *few kids* later, the last one was, in fact, a boy. Wild, huh?

God knows our todays, our tomorrows, and every day of our existence. He always has the way to our promised blessings, just like He always has the way for us to be the best ever created. They're already there, if we hold to trust and keep going to see it through. Blessings *do* come. But they don't come in order.

WHEN GOD MAKES US WAIT

Isn't it wild what we do to ourselves because of passing time? Isn't it wild all the questions that run through our mind when we feel things should have worked out by now? *Is God punishing me? Why did it have to happen to me and not them? Or why them and not me? Did I do something wrong? Why would God bring me to this just for it not to work out? What am I supposed to be learning? What is the hidden blessing from this? What tragic thing could I be avoiding from this falling through? Was it taken away because I wasn't grateful enough? Is there even divine meaning behind this, or is this just life being life? How much more am I going to go through? Is this the adversary trying to stop me, or is it God? Maybe my efforts aren't good enough. Maybe I'm not good enough. It isn't fair. It wasn't supposed to be this way.* And we think and we cry and we wonder and we plead and we pray.

Christ loved Martha, Mary, and Lazarus—one could argue that Lazarus and his two sisters were even His closest friends. When near Jerusalem, Jesus actually would spend nights sleeping at their house in Bethany and stay with the three of them. When Lazarus fell sick, Jesus heard about it but didn't go. You can imagine how confused and potentially hurt the three of them were by this, two-fold. They knew that, as the Savior, if He came, He could heal him. And secondly, they were so close—as a friend, why wouldn't He come to be with them at a time like that? When Lazarus *died,* Jesus heard about it but still didn't go. Now you can really imagine the heightened feelings of Martha and Mary. And then a day passed. And then another day passed. And then a third day passed. *Why?* I can't imagine their grief and their swirling thoughts. *This didn't have to happen, if He were here, this could have been prevented. Where is He? Why has He not come by now? Why is He not here with us? I thought He loved us?*

After years and years of priesthood blessings, we finally had our inspired move back to where I was from, New York. Everything had divinely fallen into place. The house we bought over the internet ended up being so perfect for us. Instant equity, move-in ready, completely updated, plenty of space, and only miles away from most of my family. Everything with the move was so smooth with so many miracles. I even journaled that seeing mountains move was no longer a metaphor to me, that through this process I saw literal mountains move. *Oh*, to relive my family's reaction of us at their doorstep surprising them in person after our recent and secret move, after nine years of me being across the country. One of the top highlights of my life. I even found out I was pregnant with my third, and *wow* the excitement for the first time to be around my family for my pregnancy and the birth of a child. Everyone was elated, as you can imagine. New York was needed and even better than I could have anticipated. It was *almost* perfect. Except my positive pregnancy test triggered the lingering reality that after a year of living there, we were still unemployed. Despite our tireless efforts to find work, a year had passed out there, and our old city's limited and dwindling job opportunities were not presenting themselves. Oh man, if we thought our seven months of unemployment were hard during my pregnancy with our second child, we were now reliving a terrible and trying trial and passing the time frame and making a new record: a year. (Feeling grateful now that the Lord had prepared us to both be thrifty and money savvy, to save and build up a savings account to prepare us for our unpredicted future). And yet again, I was pregnant. *How?* How is something so profoundly right, rooted years and years into my past, my blessings talking of this exact time, and we are not provided for? After years and years of inspired blessings and miracles to bring us to New York, a year later we already sold our house and were moving out of state again? How could all this buildup to this move end so quickly? Why weren't the mountains moving anymore? Why were we back to struggling and problem solving and moving? I thought He was in this with us. This was His idea.

Oh, the feelings of exhaustion are indescribable. Every day, for over three *hundred* and sixty-five days, and to have nothing to show for our efforts. Well, actually, more than that because we began looking for work a month before even leaving Utah. Indescribable wonder about what this is going to mean for our growing family becomes consuming. And not just us, but the heartbreak from my family that is even *worse* than the first time I moved nine years ago that led to years of silence from some of my family members. I dubbed me moving to Utah the hardest trial of my life. And I was quite literally reliving it again, except this time their pain was worse. Because this time I was leaving with grandkids and the unfulfilled dream of being there for the first time during pregnancy and birth and holding a newborn. I was reassured by close friends that telling my family of us leaving again would be okay and not that bad because they were my family and because it was what God wanted. But after sitting down to lunch with my dad, it really was worst-case scenario for everything we were figuring out and working toward. It was devastating and exhausting and complicated and long. Leaving me to physically ache—stretched too thin. There's a misconception that if we are doing what He wants us to, things will just "fall into place" or go smoothly, but in my personal life, that has rarely been the case. It just means that sometimes it's going to stink real bad and you just gotta do it anyway. This ongoing trial is just thickly layered with so many challenges from so many directions.

Like Mary and Martha, I find myself wondering, *Where is He? Why hasn't He arrived yet? If He truly were here with me, then why is this happening? Why wasn't this prevented? I thought He loved me.*

When I first met Ben, he was only days off of his mission. By this time, I had already graduated from college and was working a salary career. Although against what he wanted and what he envisioned as a husband and a father, when I was pregnant with my first and he was just starting school, we both felt very strongly that I needed to continue to work and he would be home with Gracie while doing online school full-time. That was *hard* for him. He really did feel like he was failing us for not working, but it didn't bother me. I knew for this time in our life, it was right, and it was just the season we were in. Six years had passed, and Ben still had waves of struggle with this. He would plead and fast over the years, hoping that our roles could change but still receiving the same answer: *not yet*. And then the time came when Gracie started preschool. She ran right in and never looked back. She slept with her backpack the night before because she was so excited and cried when it was time to go back home. And then I almost cried because I had to go to work. I don't know, ever since we potty-trained Gracie when she was two, working full-time and not being home with my kids became painful for me. I joined Ben by so desperately wishing things were different, but for right then, they couldn't be yet.

And I think of my dad having me choose him or the Church. I chose God, and my dad really had kept his word. I would call and he wouldn't answer. I'd walk to his house and he wouldn't answer. I would pray and plead and fast. *Oh,* how I fasted and cried for things to be different. I knew if I did what God wanted me to do, he would come around. But then I followed God by moving to Utah, and that made things worse with my dad. And then a year passed. And then several years had passed, and still, silence.

Going back to our first unemployment experience, when I lost my job, I embraced the change of course. I welcomed it with optimism and faith and was excited to see where this could lead to next. We put in all the effort, spiritually and physically, to find work and seek out the next opportunity. And then a month passed. And then two months passed. And then three months passed, and nothing had changed. And my optimism had faded. And my excitement had died. And after months of it all—faith and optimism and work—I figured I would have earned the trial to be over with by now. Did your eyes roll reading that? Mine did writing it. But it's how I felt. I felt I had put in all the effort for long enough that my blessing of relief of employment would have come by now. A few more months had passed even from then, and New Year's was approaching. Everyone was posting about a "new fresh start," but I was rolling my eyes thinking how much of it was really a new fresh start when I was bringing the same burden and same struggle into it with us? There's a difference between bad days and long trials, where a new day is sometimes all you need, but then we have these lingering struggles that make another day seem like a harder burden you're not sure if you can bear.

Jesus arrived in Bethany four days after Lazarus had parted. Christ first saw Martha, and she said to Him, "If thou hadst been here, my brother had not died."[17] Jesus assured her that He would rise again and that all would be well. And Martha, assuming He was referring to resurrection, agreed. But Christ corrected her with one of my favorite responses, "I *am* the resurrection, and the life."[18] Then Christ went to find Mary, who was deep in despair, and when she saw the Lord she

17. John 11:21.
18. John 11:25, emphasis added.

just collapsed at His feet and through her tears muttered, "If thou hadst been here, my brother had not died,"[19] not knowing those were the exact words Martha had said first to the Lord as well. She wept. And Jesus wept with her.

Back in the days of Jesus, culture believed that the spirit lingered around a deceased body three days after passing. So on day three, the deceased were officially *dead* dead. Had Christ come any sooner after his death, many would doubt His miracle to raise Lazarus from the grave, or even struggle to call it a miracle at all. Had Christ come sooner and prevented the death of Lazarus, many would not have been converted and they would have been shielded from the bigger miracle. A miracle so big that all the chief priests and the Pharisees held a council and said, "What do we? for this man doeth many miracles. If we let him thus alone, all men will believe on him: and the Romans shall come and take away both our place and nation."[20] A miracle so big, they knew in time, none could not believe in Christ.

After moving from New York to Arizona, unemployment continued to stretch for a total of a year and a half. Even though it really didn't seem like we would, we *did* survive both bouts of hard and ongoing unemployment and ended up, both times, with a better job with better opportunities in a different state. Mine and my husband's roles have shifted after almost seven years. And although repairs still can be made, there is no silence from my family. Of course, things are coming together. I say *of course* because when we remember who God really is, and His purpose, of course He will bring us to better things, even if on our way to them it's down a path longer than anticipated. I say *of course* because the reality is that we have made it through 100 percent of our days, because we're still here. That's what He does; it's His whole purpose for us. And like the passing time with Lazarus, He knows something we don't, if we but keep going and not pray for trials to be prevented but pray to hold out for the bigger miracles. Because blessings do not dim with passing time.

---

19. John 11:32.
20. John 11:47–48.

What I have learned from God with my honest pleadings to Him is, first, that He cares. Both as a Savior and a friend. Like Christ did with Mary, He came to me and He wept with me first. I have felt and been reminded that He is filled with love and compassion. He showed that He understood and *felt* also. That although we are on a longer than anticipated path, we are not abandoned. And He can be felt in the darkest and most confusing of times if we continue to turn to Him. I have seen that *all* that He does is fueled by that love and compassion for us. Every time I push myself to trust, I am shown that He is strategically working on our behalf and that everything we are asked to do is for a something greater, and nothing is in vain. With passing time, I have seen that everything is in its own season. Like in the story of Martha and Mary, another day may be passing, causing us to be in a long season, but seasons don't last forever.

When I had moved to Utah in my early twenties, everyone joked, saying I'd be married within months. But the years had passed after my move and I was still very single. With passing time, I started to spend my thoughts wondering what I was doing wrong. Was I not doing enough? Was there something wrong with me? Was I flawed? Was I being overlooked? Was Christ not coming to me with the bigger blessing? And then we get into that all-too-familiar dance with the adversary, when with passing time we allow him to run rogue with our thoughts. The more time that passed, the more I became consumed with it all. It took me a little while, but I did receive life-changing counsel to cope with those long seasons.

While I was thinking of Joseph Smith in Liberty Jail, it was *not* the well-quoted verse that things "shall be but a small moment" that brought me perspective but seeing how Joseph had spent his time while locked up.[21] While the Saints are suffering, the Prophet is *pleading* with the Lord for things to be over and things to be different. And what happened? Months passed, and he was still in jail. But just because time seems to be standing still doesn't mean God is. And just because we may be waiting doesn't mean that we are to be idle. I think

21. D&C 121:7.

of all the revelation Joseph Smith received while captured, the many chapters in Doctrine and Covenants that we wouldn't have if Joseph decided to shut down from his situation, if Joseph had allowed the adversary in his mind any longer with those negative thoughts that keep us standing still or moving back. That maybe it's not just about making it out alive and dragging ourselves to the end, but what if, like it was with Joseph Smith, it's about what we get *during* it all?

In my single years, I decided I was tired of wondering and doubting and time counting—what kind of living was that? I was going to worry about me and worry about God. I decided to stay focused on what really mattered to me. I worried about the relationship I *did* have: my relationship with God. I figured if we aren't doing the things we love, if we put those things on pause, we're missing the point. And that's when life started to unravel and blossom in ways I never would have imagined. I learned lessons I couldn't imagine living life without, and I grew beyond what I thought I could in such a short time. Truth is, I'm not sure what kind of wife or person I'd be without the qualities I gained, lessons I learned, and talents I developed while I was single and "waiting," because I am such a better person because of them. It was through this season, learning these things, that I started writing and I started speaking and I started to become who I am today and who I know I was meant to be, and who God intended me to be all along.

When I was waiting to get endowed on my own, my bishop told me that I couldn't do anything different but that the timing just wasn't right. That made things harder to hear, that I was ready but the timing wasn't right. He told me what he tells to all missionaries who are leaving later than intended for whatever reason, "I look forward to the day I get an email from you when you're out in the mission field telling me of an experience you had where you knew you were exactly right where you needed to be for that to happen." Just a short year later, when I did end up getting endowed on my own, I was walking out of the temple for the first time and it was then that my dad called *just to talk and to tell me he loved me* for the first time in a long time. It was then I knew that I was exactly where I needed to be when I needed to be there, and the wait suddenly seemed profound.

If we are trying and a trial hasn't ended yet, decide to be productive with your time, actively seek out lessons and opportunities. Move forward with the things you know you should be doing and what God wants you to do. Move forward knowing that though we wonder why He hasn't arrived yet and why we weren't protected, God knows something we don't. Something better.

There will always be something to overcome, something hard to handle, or something new to figure out. How unproductive it is to long for the trial to be over, to crave a fast-forward button, to hang on to that make-believe mortal vision we create in our minds. Turn anger and confusion into productive experiences that allow you to grow in the greatest ways. Having that mindset will chase away anger or bitterness and turn your trying times into productive learning and growing times. We're allowed to feel deflated, we're allowed to struggle, we're allowed to feel sad or upset. But it's up to us whether or not to choose to live there. The adversary will stay as long as we allow him to. But we have the literal power to cast him out, a power he has to obey.

If we are trying, we will never be asked to go through things that wouldn't be for the best. Lessons and growth are there. God is there. Things may not go the way we want and pray for them to, but they will always be profoundly better than what we even knew was available for ourselves. Sometimes we can't help but think how much easier it would be if things had gone the way we wanted them to go. But little do we know what's right around the corner for us when we choose to remember God—opportunities that await, the people, the growth, and the blessings. Because, truly, the best things come from God.

Just because things haven't worked out yet doesn't mean they won't. Promised blessings don't expire. Passing time can't dim blessings promised to us. Write them down, remember them, and hang out for a wild adventure with lessons and experiences you wouldn't ever trade. Don't allow passing time to bring doubt or cause you to settle. Don't lose patience and miss out on what He has in store for you. And in the meantime, don't hold yourself back from learning and growing and experiencing other things. Just hold on, and don't lose confidence. Heavenly Father knows what's important to us and what we need.

Do not let time and trials dim your faith or diminish the truthfulness of His promises to you. Never lose confidence. His promises are so real. There are far, far better things ahead, I promise. God promises. That's what I love about Him—you will never be shortchanged from the best blessings ever. Your prayers have been heard, but *greater* are the things He has in store for you. Receive the unexpected but profoundly greater path with the best blessings.

None of our effort and none of our faith is in vain. When we wonder why, remember the counsel given to the Prophet Joseph Smith in Liberty Jail, "The Son of Man hath descended below them all. Art thou greater than he? Therefore, hold on thy way."[22] Because truly, it all will seem like a small moment, because life here is like a tiny little bead in the middle of a never-ending string, going infinitely to the left, all that happened before we came here, and infinitely to the right, all that is to come next. Sometimes we don't always know the what, but we do always know the *who*. And I'm all in for whatever is to come next!

---

22. D&C 122:8–9.

CHAPTER 5

When God Is Silent

BEN AND I HAD AN AWESOME MORNING BREAKFAST to-
gether with great conversation. We usually have typical, awesome
mornings, and this day was no different. Soon after eating, he left to
drop off packages at the post office. I was crawling under our table
picking up things that fell off the table from the kids, and as soon as
the door closed behind him, I unconsciously burst into tears. I sat un-
derneath our dining room table and cried an ugly cry for twenty whole
minutes. What a sight that was. So there I was, alone. Under my table. Hysterical. Clearly, I was doing great at life in this moment. You'd
think with all the challenges life brings, I'd learn how to avoid situations like this. Maybe you have, but I haven't.

Honestly, I was glad Ben wasn't there. Not because I was embar-
rassed or because he would have judged me or anything like that. But I
think the weight of my current to-do list was too heavy that I was just
too tired and too overwhelmed to try and explain it in words. I was
glad he wasn't there because I didn't think I could explain it in a way
that he would really understand. In this moment, I was alone—physically alone, but also alone in my challenge. Alone knowing even if I
were to try and explain it, it wouldn't fully be grasped or understood,
and it definitely would not be felt the way I was feeling it.

And we have these moments, right? When we feel alone. Literally and/or emotionally. And we are certain that no matter our efforts, there's no way to properly express to anyone what we're really feeling. Challenges stink, regardless. But feeling by yourself in them is what makes them even more difficult. As I was crying thinking of deadlines I was about to miss and feeling the reality of a positive pregnancy test I took the night before for our third child, my mind was racing. *I really can't do this.* Praying, if we could call it that, but mostly yelling at God for twenty minutes straight, demanding to know how. I started doubting my ability and myself in general. *Am I cut out for this? Strong enough? Am I crumbling? What's life going to look like now? Am I losing myself? Is God really behind all this? Is this God's path for me— under my table completely weighed down with too many questions about the journey ahead of me? Is His path always going to feel this heavy and lonely?*

After venting, I listened. I desperately tried to pay attention to anything that would pop into my head, hoping it was God answering me. And I thought of the man with palsy. But maybe not in the way that you would think.

The man with palsy desperately wanted to get to Jesus to be healed, and we know he does. But he couldn't get to Christ himself, quite literally. He needed to be carried and physically brought to Him. And what a night he chose!

Jesus was at Peter's house that day, and apparently it was the place to be, because there were so many people at Peter's house at this time that they couldn't all fit inside. There were floods of people even outside surrounding it. It was an action-packed night among so many friends that there was little room for movement. Ah, but the man with palsy had a group of choice friends who were so determined for him to get closer to the Savior and receive the comfort he wanted that they carried him in on a stretcher. But when they arrived and still couldn't get to Christ because of this multitude at the house, they all pulled this man up to the roof of Peter's house. They then peeled off clay tiles on Peter's roof to make a hole big enough that a grown man in a stretcher could fit through, and then they lowered him down. How's that for a visual of love and support from those around you?

Ben came home, and although no longer crying, I was still on the floor with the craziest hair and the reddest eyes and obvious not-quite-dried snot on the sleeve of my sweatshirt. Neither of us said or asked anything. He just . . . crawled under the table next to me. And he rubbed my back. He met me where I was and comforted and lifted me. And then I was reminded of the all too many times when this exact thing has happened. It's laughable how many times this same thing has happened, maybe not under a table, but him coming to me in my tears. Or how many times it was his sweatshirt that had my snot drying on the sleeve and all the prayers he has said over my challenges. What a cycle.

And then it hit me. Not only did I not need to explain myself, and I wasn't actually alone, but like the man with Palsy, I got myself a good support system who is determined to see me heal and succeed and move closer to Christ. And perhaps it's correct he doesn't know exactly what I'm feeling, but who says that's a qualifying factor when he, like the man with palsy's friends, knows where I want to go? Oh, how important it is to have those people there for us when we feel we do not have words to call out for help. Those crippling moments that leave us debilitated in our tracks. Oh, how important it is to seek after and cultivate these determined friendships that will literally lift us up. Even if it feels as though we are dead weight on a stretcher, they carry us. They are determined to see us be healed and succeed and make steps closer to the Savior at those times when we feel we cannot do it ourselves. Do we have people like that in our lives right now? Do adjustments need to be made? Do more efforts need to be made? It is worth the effort.

But sometimes it's not always like that. I didn't always have my husband, and there was a long period of time, years and years, I didn't have any friends at all, let alone close friends. What then? Who then?

What of the time when, because of my decision to get baptized, every single one of my friends wanted nothing to do with me and what I was a part of? And how badly that hurt because of how easy it was for them to leave, and how quickly they did leave. What of the time when, because of my decision to get baptized, my best friend and biggest support—my dad—said he didn't want me as a daughter anymore? What of the time God told me to leave my family and move across the country to a state I'd never been to, where I didn't know a single person? What of the time when I moved to a new state by myself, and when people took one look at me, they would walk the opposite direction? And the eight years of living by myself with no roommates, when no one could walk in on me crying under a table? What about the times when I fell asleep on the floor, in the position I was crying in the night before, because no one was there to come to me?

And what of times not only of physical loneliness, but times when I felt alone spiritually? Unanswered prayers. Unfulfilled fasts. Passing time. Unwanted and uncharted paths. Times when I felt things got worse from following the Spirit. Times when I felt I was being punished for doing what I thought was the right thing. Times when I have pleaded to feel the Spirit and I just didn't in that moment. Times when I felt lost, and out of sight of God. A stranger. Alone. Unnamed and unimportant.

Those are hard realities. That is a heavy weight that is very real. But although the effects of feeling those things are real, being hidden from and out of sight of God is not. Though those feelings are real, it is up to us to stay there or not, to remember the character of God or allow the adversary to run rogue with that thought, and we end up hiding ourselves—not God hiding from us. And we mourn and "refuse to be comforted."[23]

Maybe the woman at the well, as she sat alone drawing water, was thinking of the weight of her burdens. Maybe she was thinking about how she wished she could change things and how she wished things were different. Perhaps she was thinking of how she was only there because she wanted to be alone. Or maybe because she deserved to be alone.

---

23. Ether 15:3.

There was a straight shot shortcut to Galilee through the Beth-shan gap. It was essentially the only route for Jews to travel for two reasons: (1) it was fastest, and (2) the longer route would mean they would have to travel through Samaria, a city that descended from heathen colonists (in short, they hated Jews). So not only was the route through Samaria longer, but they would have to travel through a city they avoided due to deep hatred. But Christ journeyed that route purposely. And that's when He met the woman at the well. The disciples were shocked that He even spoke to her, a Samaritan. And not just a Samaritan, but a sinful woman of a hated and despised apostate race. And not only did he talk to her; he taught her and stayed with her there for two days.

So yeah, we may feel alone and burdened. We may be under our table or we may be at a well, but regardless of what and where, Jesus will and does travel the "long way" to get to us. On purpose. Even, and especially, when everyone else may fail us. He meets us where we are and comforts and lifts us. He comes to us because He doesn't lose sight of us. Because He knows our hiding places. "Because they are not lost to God. He knows where they are."[24] Regardless of what we have done or haven't done, regardless if we are tirelessly trying to do what's right or on a long road of shortcomings and sins, He comes to us. And He stays with us. And what we think is a painful moment alone with a weight we wouldn't know how to explain to anyone else could turn into an intimate one-on-one moment with the Savior, if, like the woman at the well, we are willing to listen and if we are willing to be taught.

But how? How could that be for someone like me? I mean, who am I? What if I'm the exception? What if I haven't earned His love yet? Or what if I weakened it? we ask. But those questions stem from the biggest lie and misconception, that God's love is inconsistent. Here's the truth: we do not have to earn His love. Should that be on a line on its own? Definitely.

We *do not* earn His love.

---

24. 3 Nephi 17:4.

Maybe we are earning His trust. And earning the better blessings. But we are never earning His love. That's already there. When we hear that God is an unchanging God, we think that means just His commandments are unchanging. But that also means His love. His love for us in unchanging, never weakening, always there. *How?* Well, because we are His. He loves us because we are His. And *how much* does He love us? Even as much as He has "graven thee upon the palms of [His hands]."[25]

When we look at every scripture reference of healing and forgiveness and miracles, it was always individual and personal. The children that ran to Christ when He visited America. When He asked those afflicted in any way to feel the prints in His hands. The woman at the well. Me under my table. Because we really are His, that alone makes us enough. We are His, and that is everything. And unlike my husband, and unlike those in our lives, no matter how resilient and dedicated they are to us, Jesus actually does know. Exactly and perfectly does He know what we're going through, and He does know what we're feeling, without explanation. He knows all of us because He created all of us.[26]

Then why does He feel distant from us sometimes? Why do we feel as though we sometimes cannot feel or see? Why does it seem sometimes that our time at the well alone drawing water has been too long and maybe He's not coming?

For the second year in a row, but in different states, I had my husband sneak out during sacrament meeting and tape a gold star to the wall of our classroom because he is taller and can get it higher up than I could. The star was the size of my hand. I began teaching my Christmas lesson, and near the end of the hour I asked if anyone had noticed the star in the room. And in the two years of doing this, no one ever had. It wasn't hidden. It was just to the left of them, by itself. But just because they didn't see it doesn't change the fact that it was there. And similarly, even though many did not notice the star when Christ was born, that doesn't change the fact that He was.

---

25. 1 Nephi 21:16.
26. See Alma 18:32.

A few years ago, I was speaking at Time Out for Girls in Salt Lake City. It was a two-day conference for teen girls with about four thousand girls in attendance. It was toward the end of the second day while another speaker was on stage. She told all the girls to close their eyes. "Raise your hand if you felt the Spirit this weekend," she said. My eyes weren't closed, and I watched the hand of every single girl go up. *Amazing*, I thought.

While their eyes were still closed, the speaker said, "Raise your hand if you feel like you've never felt God." And then I watched hands go up. The same hands that had just been raised in recognition to feeling the Spirit. *Wait.*

They got it all mixed up. There's a big disconnect. They didn't make the connection that the Spirit is the tool God uses to communicate to us. They didn't realize that when they felt the Spirit, they were quite literally feeling God. They didn't realize that those notes they took in their journals were what God wanted them to know and focus on right then, that He was talking to them the whole weekend, speaking, answering, guiding. They didn't realize that those times when their hearts were beating a little faster, that was God. Those times that they laughed or felt comforted or felt added hope, that was God communicating with them directly.

Sometimes we get it a little skewed. It's easy to feel disconnected when we forget all the different ways God comes to us. And surely, when it's not in our expected way, how easy it is to say He is not there at all, that we are the exception to His "one by one" rule we read and hear about. We hear testimonies in sacrament meetings of miracles and think, *I've never felt that or received an answer like that. I must be doing something wrong. I must not be good enough. He must not be there for me because He doesn't speak to me or come to me the way I hear He does to others.*

As the pioneers were traveling west, one night in particular was counted terrible among the many bad. It was a night of destruction and hatred where these tired and sacrificing saints were assaulted, murdered, driven out at gunpoint, and chased in the middle of the freezing night, separated from their few belongings, their horses if they were lucky to have one, and more tragically, their family members. They were forced off course and into the freezing Missouri River to escape their potential death. Thousands of Latter-day Saints were stuck in mud, terrified, hungry, wet, and freezing, but they knew that if they were to turn back, the mob would kill them. Where was God in this? Where was God in their sacrifice? Where was God in the course of them following the Spirit? God's path? Where were their answered prayers of protection and safety? Ah, isn't it a little too true to be funny that those are usually the first questions we ask ourselves? Isn't it wild how subtle and smooth the adversary is?

And just as the Saints were close to consumed with those questions and that doubt and pain and abandonment from God, a shooting star lit up the sky. And then another. And then another. In fact, there were so many shooting stars happening at the same time that it lit up the entire sky, endless meteors! Innumerable meteors shooting from every direction! Some reports estimated exceeding 100,000 per hour, and others guessed thirty flashes per second. The fiery show lasted throughout the entire night. It was so awe-inspiring that the intended mass slaughter planned for that following night, when the Saints were unprotected easy targets, was disassembled because those in the mob themselves were captivated in their tracks. God, in His vastness, brought forth beauty amidst darkness to show that He was still there with them. That He was mindful. That they were not alone in this and their faith was not in vain.

The adversary confuses us in the best way he does, subtly masked as "logic," we justify in our heads. We lose sight of God and His vastness of goodness. We've narrowed Him down to only a few adjectives and unconsciously dismissed the rest. We forget or dismiss or, like in my Christmas lesson, not notice everything else. Maybe people were looking for a baby to know Christ was born and not a star. Maybe we are so focused on looking for a resolution that we miss the shooting stars He sends.

And so we have life and all that goes with it, seasons of enjoyment and comfort or seasons of uncharted paths and unwanted situations and moments of darkness and chaos. And though He doesn't always take away the chaos and darkness, He always comes to us to show us He is there for us. That we aren't alone. And that our faith and our efforts are not in vain. How wise it would be to interrupt our readily available doubts and negative questions and to then rethink God and His characteristics and all the many ways He shows us He is there for us. I wonder what we will find if we but take the time to look.

All good things come from God. Including feelings. Every feeling of happiness, every feeling of comfort, every feeling of hope. Every feeling of forgiveness. Of strength. Of laughter. Of lifted weight. Of protection. Change. Every feeling of guidance is from and because of God. Every thought we have, even if fleeting, that tells us we can make it through another day, to just hold out a little longer and to keep going. Moments when we think, *Ah, okay!* Those moments that we can't really explain, moments when our hearts beat just a little bit faster. Goose bumps moments. Moments when we feel our eyes water and we know if we blink, tears will fall. Moments when we feel our souls jolt and dance within us.

No, maybe He doesn't come and take our situation away, and maybe He doesn't come in the way we were hoping and expecting, but good will always be there because God really is always there. But like the star when Christ was born, and like the star in my classroom, and like the many, many ways He tries to get our attention every day, just because we may not see them doesn't mean they are not there. Just because they may be different doesn't mean that He is not there.

In contrast, this should make it easier to recognize the adversary. It's crucial to know how the adversary works so we can catch him in his snares and abandon him and not God, so we can perform and live better without the unnecessary doubt and weight slowing us down. A good indicator of the adversary's work is if something makes you feel bad, negative, or down—that is not the Spirit. It's the adversary that makes us feel anything that is not good. It's the adversary that stops us or slows us down from growing into the successful, thriving person God intended us to become all along. If it is not good, it is not God. Anything that brings us away from God is Satan's itinerary. Are your questions and actions bringing you closer to or further away from doing what we have been taught to do? Do we have thoughts that tell us we are alone? Thoughts that we cannot turn to God because He doesn't care about us, or that we are not worthy enough to? Thoughts of what's the point of praying if my situation does not go how I am asking? Those are not characteristic of God, because God is good. Even when our lives need correcting, it is never done in such a way to discourage us, but to build us up and motivate us. With correction coming from God, it comes coupled with reassurance and hope and comfort, rather than the contrast, of shame or hopelessness. The sooner we can recognize the adversary, the faster we can cast Him out—a literal power that is ours, a power he has to obey. And then we can experience just a little deeper just how beautiful and dedicated our Father in Heaven really is.

Elder Holland requests, "Believe in miracles. I have seen so many of them come when every other indication would say that hope was lost. Hope is *never* lost. If those miracles do not come soon or fully or seemingly at all, remember the Savior's own anguished example: if the bitter cup does not pass, drink it and be strong, trusting in happier days ahead."[27]

As we move forward, even if with the smallest of steps, our efforts will not only be noticed, but they will be magnified. And until our big miracle comes that brings us to have our turn in sacrament meeting, recognize the unexpected, yet still real, little ones. And in those times when it is harder to feel or to see, think of those times when you have felt them. Because regardless of how subtle and crafty the adversary is, I refuse to let some pathetic attempt by him take away from the reality of the times when I truly did in reality feel God. Because although sometimes I have these trials that leave me wondering and hoping for more from Him, I can't let that moment take away from every single time He has delivered me previously.

---

27. "Like a Broken Vessel," *Ensign*, Nov. 2013.

Can you think of a time when you've felt the Spirit? Can you think of a time when you've felt hope? Peace? Love, forgiveness, happiness, laughter, comfort?

Yeah, maybe we do that all-too-familiar dance with the adversary, but then we have these moments in our life when we feel and experience, so deeply, that we have no words to describe exactly what happened or how we felt . . . but we just know that *electrifying* feeling is from God and from this gospel. And I refuse to let the adversary's pathetic attempts take away from all those times when I in reality did feel God. I refuse to let the adversary take away from the reality of those times I have felt the good. When I have felt my soul dancing within me.

In times of wonder, I think to myself, *He has helped me before; He will help me again. He has listened in the past; He will listen again. He has blessed me before; He will bless me again. He has come to me before; He will come again.*

Remembering that our God is an unchanging God and recognizing that it doesn't just refer to commandments will help us discover the reality that our "one by one" God will always be, and that will not change. And the fact that our unchanging God is exactly that, *un*changing, means that our helping God will always be a helping God. That our God will always be a God of miracles. Of mercy. Of guidance. Of revelation. The fact that our unchanging God is unchanging means that His love for His children is also unchanging. Our God will always be a loving God who is bound to His promises to us if we are trying in any degree. And "surely the thing God enjoys most about being God is the *thrill* of being merciful, especially to those who don't expect it and often feel they don't deserve it."[28] And that will also never change. If we but stay close to Him and look, we find what we look for. And it may be tempting to focus on the hard and the hurt and the confusion, but remember, that's the adversary's snare. If we look, we will find God with His arms wide open in the opportunity, in the comfort, in the answers, in the love extended and the love felt, in the glimmers of

---

28. "The Laborers in the Vineyard," *Ensign*, May 2012, emphasis added.

hope, in the friend who reached out, the laughter, the happy tears shed at girls camp, the racing heart during sacrament meeting, and in the strength to make it one more day.

I hope every day we will remember His unchanging promise to us that He will not leave us comfortless. That we are never alone. And that He does travel the long way to us and sit with us one on one. Because we are His, and that always makes us enough.

CHAPTER 6

When It's Not
What We Wanted

G ROWING UP WELL LOVED AND CONFIDENT, Joseph in
the Old Testament was excited about the future he had. With
visions of being a leader and with parents who favored him, it definitely seemed like justified excitement for the path he was to live. *Life
was good.* Until it wasn't. Escaping talk of potentially being murdered
by his own brothers, Joseph was instead abandoned in a hole and that
good life had now been robbed from him. With great confusion about
why this was happening to him and what he did to deserve this, he
soon found that things were about to get much worse. He was sold as
a slave to Egypt. As Joseph tried to keep his integrity and work hard
and things were starting to look up, he took another blow. He was imprisoned because of the deceit of others. And then a year passed. And
then *another* year passed. And there Joseph was, still in prison. This
was most definitely not the life he wanted to live. And this was most
definitely not the life he felt he was promised to live either.

Thinking life was actually pretty great already, I knew entering
in through the gate of joining the Church and making covenants was
only going to make it better. I was elated with the cards dealt to me in
life because I learned that God is real, and I am His. I learned I can talk

directly to the most powerful being to ever exist and that He is a God who keeps His promises if I keep trying. *Life was good.* Until it wasn't.

Skipping over losing friends and family, I think of the night when I was so excited to tell God about my decision to serve a mission. It was a conversation I knew He'd approve of and give me the green light to begin working toward. And we already know the answer I got: move to Utah. I retell this experience because it was the first time I experienced an unwanted and unexpected redirection from God. I was rerouted in a completely different direction with something not only undesirable but foreign to me. I completely forgot Utah was even a state until I met all these missionaries! I didn't know anyone there, I'd never been there before . . . Why would this even be an option for me?

I started thinking that perhaps since this was God's idea, I'd start to see the fruits of the great life I was promised. When I had gotten there and was welcomed with grief and sacrifice and loss and judgment and harder trials, I couldn't help but feel like Joseph. This is not what I wanted and this is not what I felt I was promised. And like him, I tried. I really tried to keep going and figure it out and hold on to my integrity and what I thought I should be doing and who I thought I should be. Turns out my journey to the West seemed like my journey to a hole in the ground, my something worse.

I think of the time we were planning a move to Arizona, my favorite state to ever exist. It was a move we felt God was allowing to happen, and so we moved forward with planning and didn't renew our lease to where we were living. It wasn't until we had to be out that we were told that Arizona was to happen, *but not yet.* Ben and I had a distinct impression to temporarily move into and rent a basement space to help close ones out financially until it was time for our out-of-state move. I knew it was right because the idea was reoccurring to both of us, but I really fought this. From the age of seventeen I'd lived completely on my own with no roommates, and here I was married and having just birthed our first child a few weeks ago, and I felt I was moving backward in life. But, mind you, this wasn't a "basement apartment," because this wasn't even an apartment at all. It wasn't actually even a basement hardly at all because it wasn't finished. And by "wasn't finished," I actually mean it wasn't even a *started* basement.

There was no bathroom. No running water. The entire floor and perimeter walls were cement. There were actually no walls or rooms at all, just wooden beams where a wall was supposed to maybe one day go, leaving it all open space of a cellar. No real ceiling, just pink insulation. There was no natural light, just those little rectangle windows at the very top by the ceiling. There was no separate door to enter. We had two very large dogs at the time, and we had furniture stacked so the dogs, and sometimes us, would come in and out through the window. We were there for the winter and living in a cement cellar—it was a *cold* winter. We really did spend most nights with hand warmers in our socks, and sometimes I'd fall asleep with them on my nose. How is any of this part of a progressing life? What kind of life was I bringing our first child into? What part of this was part of a better life I thought I was promised? I just asked my husband what he had to say about our time in the basement, and after a series of bad facial expressions and horizontal headshakes, he said, "The basement was an unfortunate situation that I'm not sure looking back how we got through it." I have been in too many metaphorical holes as I reflect on every trial I've ever gone through, but this time my hole wasn't metaphorical anymore. Was this needed? Why did this need to be part of my journey? Because at that time, all that seemed like something pulling me further away from living a better life.

I think of when we finally made it to Arizona, it was even better than I ever dreamed it would be. I was *made* for dry heat and hot summers with scorching sunshine and cactuses. I found my best version of me out there. Even my bad days didn't seem that bad because I would just step outside and see palm trees and have my reason to cheer up. Ben and I were swimming once, and I vividly remember telling him, "If God will let us, I'll stay here forever!" And *this* is when our first bout of unemployment that I mentioned earlier came. You know about the long passing time of no progress. You know of the tireless prayers and fasts and pleadings to find work and it just didn't happen. You know of the depleting bank account and the no health insurance while expecting our second baby. I didn't think this trial could have affected us any more negatively than it already did. Until it did. With only a few hundred dollars left in our account and only a month left in my pregnancy, I got an offer for a job that I didn't even apply to. It was a job that would be paying more than double what I was making before I was laid off, and they would relocate us so we wouldn't have to invest our last little bit to get there, although I don't think we had enough to make it there on our own anyway. You may be thinking, *Wow, great blessing and answer to seven months of prayers,* but I didn't see it that way. I was desperate to accept anything *except this*. Because *this* was going to rip me away from Arizona. Because this was going to rip me away from what set my soul dancing! The trial had already taken so much from us, and now it was going to take away what I so desperately loved. Yet again, something so important to me was going to be ignored and unfulfilled and then sacrificed. So then is God not powerful enough to stop it or not loving enough to stop it?

"Could it be that because I have been so afraid, so busy pushing God away, I am living beneath God's privilege for me? What if there is a well—a reservoir of blessings—that I have not yet approached because I have been so careful about keeping God at arm's length?"[29] Had these experiences and so many more caused me to unconsciously keep God at arm's length? Was I allowing myself to become so rugged by the unexpected that perhaps I was holding myself back from better things?

But then I thought of Joseph and how all of his series of unwanted and even worse panned out for him. How did his hole to slavery to prison end up for him? Did his life continue in the pattern of unwanted to *getting worse*? Did his life continue in what seemed like a series of missed blessings, missed potential, missed promises, and ignored desires?

Using his God-given gifts to interpret the king's dreams, Joseph did in fact become a leader, just as he always felt he would be. He led the entire people through being productive in their posterity and being smart

---

29. Emily Belle Freeman, *Even This: Getting to the Place Where You Can Trust God with Anything* (Shadow Mountain, 2017), 77.

and prepared in their famine. After seeing all his trials through, Joseph told his brothers to not be afraid. He knew that God had intended this for him all along. That through it all, his trials—the hole, the slavery, the prison—had led him to greater things that were intricately part of it all to begin with.

His promises of a great life with great blessings, his vision of being a leader . . . all of it was not only fulfilled, but magnified! Instead of being a leader of his small area over his own family, he was magnified and became a leader over all of Egypt! He literally saved an entire civilization. And not only was he reunited with his family, but he was able to bring all of them to something better, a better way of living on better and more land with a more abundant life. It was in every sense the ultimate magnification. God was not overlooking or ignoring or punishing, but in fact, He was working hard with every little detail to be sure it was *even better* than what Joseph had in mind. All of it had been part of the plan to begin with, needed and necessary and perfectly crafted for him at every stage and in every season and in every *even worse* moment.

So is He not powerful enough to stop it, or is He not loving enough to stop it? Neither. Not contradicting but opposite. Because truly, "all things have been done in the wisdom of him who knoweth all things."[30] It's easier to see this with Joseph because we can see his mortal life from start to end. But we can't see that with ours. All we may be seeing right now is us in a hole. Or us feeling imprisoned. It's hard knowing our desires are not His will—that's usually when we feel cheated. It's then that fear comes in. It's then that we have all the questions about if He actually cares about us, if He's really a part of the details, if promises will be fulfilled. It's hard because we don't know where any of it will lead us. What if we don't like where He brings us? If I were in charge and if things went my way, then I would be able to control unmet expectations and disappointments. I feel safer when I am in charge of my own life because it's comfortable knowing and being in charge. But what would we do differently about our now if we could see our end like we see Joseph's?

---

30. 2 Nephi 2:24.

I was driving to my chiropractor, and when I was at a complete stop at a red light, someone coming off the freeway ramp drove full force into the back of me, which caused me to hit the car in front of me, and, ironically, I suffered extreme double whiplash. Luckily no one was seriously injured, but I did have a badly bruised leg and a rescheduled chiropractor appointment for my neck, at which we found out two of my vertebrae were smashed on top of each other. Because my hands were on the steering wheel during impact, I couldn't lift my arms at all or move them too much in general. I had a fireside the following day, and they had to announce that I wasn't able to hug anyone and to be gentle touching me when meeting me—haha. We were hoping that our car could be salvaged, but it was totaled. *Ugh.* I was annoyed with the insurance process and having to invest in buying a new car, and then the craziest thing happened: this car accident became one of the greatest things to ever happen to us.

Apparently, we were ignorantly part of a really bad scam when we went from leasing our car to buying it. And we had no idea. So when our car was totaled, we learned that even after four years of on-time high payments, we owed *more* money than what we bought the car for. Because of that, this car accident ended up being a huge miracle that helped us avoid being in a huge financial mess for a *really* long time. And yet my first reaction was to doubt God's hand in my life and wonder how this could happen. I can now see this particular unwanted event from start to end, and here I am saying it is one of the greatest things to happen to us. I wonder just how different I'd be if I saw my whole life from start to end like this car accident.

I realize just how many times I'm Sariah, Lehi's wife. I think I have been her in just about every single situation that didn't go how I planned. Sariah had faith to pursue her something different and un-wanted and unexpected, and she showed that faith by agreeing to pack up and leave their home and wander into the wilderness. She did it. The Lord commanded, and she obeyed. But then the passing time stretched on and on. And then the unrest and questions and worries and doubt came with it. As time passed and Sariah and her family were still in the wilderness, she began to wonder about their counsel to "go and do,"[31] and she began to become afraid for their lives and the outcome.

The Lord commanded me to go to Utah over a mission, and I obeyed. The Lord commanded we move into an unfinished basement, and we obeyed. The Lord commanded me to give up Arizona, and I moved. And every single time I allowed it out of my control and into His, my reaction was fear and unconscious distrust. I have faith to pursue, but like Sariah, once I'm in it I psych myself out when things don't make sense right away or things don't add up quite yet or the unwanted path is longer than anticipated.

We begin to murmur. But what does murmur even mean in modern days? It's easy to spot it in scriptures, but maybe it's because we aren't the ones going through it. Or maybe because we already know the outcome of and reason for what is being asked because we already see the start and the end.

But modern-day murmuring is different. It's hidden behind and masked as concern or logic or passion. We unconsciously counsel the Lord about what we think is best based off of the information we have been given as our personal part in the world. I remember how interesting going online was when President Nelson announced an official shift to refer to ourselves by the full name of our church. Seems little, right? It wasn't. Many really struggled with it. *Why* this? *Why right now? Why not* that? *Couldn't time and resources be spent on better things? There's so much the Brethren don't understand about how much this is going to affect things for the worse, like online marketing!* There were a lot of confused people, but there were also a lot of hurt people. People hurt that a different announcement or update hadn't been made, one that would have impacted them directly or answered their personal prayers and desires.

It's interesting, living in the times that we do. We all know things we need to stray from and avoid because of the historical examples in the scriptures. But like the famous quote on pride, we rarely see it in ourselves. It's all masked by our understanding that our feelings are our realities, and our realities can't be wrong. *Right?*

---

31. See 1 Nephi 3:7.

I understand quite clearly now that those who murmured and were "unrighteous" in scriptures probably didn't feel like they were "wicked" in the moment. Perhaps just confused. Or hurt. Or simply being logical about what makes perfect human sense.

But we can't see the start and the end; we can only see the *past* and the *now* and the *where we want to go,* and we base our realities on that. It's hard because the Spirit isn't always logical. It's *spiritual.* Which means our brains sometimes won't have that understanding. Our lack of full understanding mixed with our personal desires brings looking beyond the mark.

And I cannot get the quote from Elder Uchtdorf out of mind, when he asks if we really need to follow all the Lord reveals and says, "I think God knows something we don't."[32] And *all that the Lord reveals and asks of us* doesn't only mean commandments and revelations to the prophet and Church, but also what He asks of us individually in our personal lives, whether it be moving to a basement or a different state, or whether it be being abandoned in a hole.

Looking beyond the mark is a warning in scriptures and a warning over general conference pulpits. But, *gah,* how hard it is to see when our priorities and our passions are not the same as the Lord's priorities. I get that. I struggle continually with that. But looking beyond the mark is a subtle snare the adversary does to really pull us away from progress and growth with God and the separation of the world's ways from His ways.

Maybe instead of being like Sariah, we can be more like the sons of Helaman. Everything about their situation made no *logical* sense. There were only 2,000 of them, and they were supposed to defend themselves, their people, and their entire country. The enemy was *innumerable.* They were severely outnumbered and the odds were not in their favor, and nothing logically showed that they should have survived. While suffering "great afflictions of every kind,"[33] they knew

---

32. "Living the Gospel Joyful," *Ensign,* Nov. 2014.
33. Alma 56:16.

their God was with them and that "he will not suffer that we should fall; then let us go forth."[34] And not only did they survive; they also won. And maybe it was because even without seeing the end, they "did not fear," and they "did not doubt."[35] And even when it seems like we are fighting and struggling and the odds aren't in our favor, like them, if we hold to faith and confidence instead of distrust and doubt, then we too can overcome "as if with the strength of God."[36] Can we be like the stripling warriors and not like Sariah, and not just believe in Him but trust Him even *during battle*? During our hole and slavery and prison moments? We may have the faith to be healed and spared and helped right here and now, but do we have the faith to *not*?

I found myself saying, "God is so good," after finally hearing good news about my third pregnancy. But was God still good all the times I left after hearing bad news? Was He still good after I received a high-risk diagnostic? Was He still good after continued and unfolding complications? Was God still good even when things were not? Was He still good during all of my other trials, along all the unwanted paths I've walked, and during the times miracles didn't come for me?

When sharing my medical miracle with others, I found myself feeling weird by the phrases we often give in response to miracles or survival, such as "Oh, angels were definitely with you!" Or, "Oh, God was definitely watching over you!"

What of those who don't make it? What of those who don't receive the wanted miracle or healing or continued life? Were angels not with them? Were they abandoned and unfavored by God? Did He just not love them as much as others? Or is God just not always good? I'm bothered by those phrases, because what it implies goes against the truths of God.

The reality is, through the good and the bad, God does not play favorites. Through the good and the bad, the wanted and unwanted,

---

34. Alma 56:46.
35. Alma 56:47.
36. Alma 56:56.

through surviving or passing to the next phase, He does not turn His back, nor does He close His eyes, neglect, or abandon us.

The reality is, the biggest miracle we are trying to attain is not prevention. If we were working toward prevention, then Christ would have come immediately when he heard Lazarus was sick, because He had the ability to heal him. Instead, He consciously waited and allowed him to die.

If it were about avoidance and prevention, then the bigger miracle would have never happened—raising Lazarus from the dead. A miracle so big that all the chief priests and Pharisees held a council and asked, "What do we? for this man doeth many miracles. If we let him thus alone, all men will believe on him." A miracle so big that they knew, in time, no one could *not* believe in Christ.

If it were about avoidance and prevention, then what of Christ's life? Was His life of being mocked and falsely judged and murdered a result of angels not being there? Was it because God was not mindful of Him? Was it because God is not always good? Perhaps one of my favorite verses for perspective is when God Himself is referenced: "It pleased the Lord to bruise Him." Why? Because there was, in fact, something so much more to come.

So, what if we got it all backward? What if every step is the miracle?

Like Christ sleeping on the boat during the raging storm, it was not because he was not mindful, or that he didn't care. He knew that all would be well, regardless of the storm, because He knew that His Father was there. He is in charge, He is leading, and He is perfect.

God was good even when I got bad news from the doctors. God is good even during unwanted circumstances, in missed opportunities, and through passing time. Good because He keeps His promises.

He is good both in continued life and in passing. He is good because He is aware, He is conscious, and He is actively a part of every detail of our spirits. And He does not play favorites. God is good because we are a part of something so much bigger than our narrow-mindedness. So much bigger than what's here. Not abandoning or overlooking, He is intricately and profoundly involved in bringing us to what's next. And whatever that may be, He is there. He is in charge, He is leading, and He is perfect.

God is good even when our situation is not, because He knows something we don't. Because there is, in fact, something so much more to come.

"The Lord our God *did* visit us *with assurances* that he would deliver us; yea, insomuch that he did speak peace to our souls, and did grant unto us great faith, and did cause us that we should hope for our deliverance in him."[37] He may not take away our situations or make sense of the logical odds, but when we continue on the path He has asked of us, especially those unplanned ones He brings us to, He will come to us. He will give us assurances to show us He is still there and aware and all will, in fact, work out. We may not see the end, but He does. And He knows something we don't.

There has been something profound and needed at every stage in every trial in every season I have gone through. Nothing is ever fully doom and gloom because even in the midst of unwanted and even in the transition of *getting worse* and even in what seems an ignored desire that is important, God is there. Not ignoring and not punishing but filled with comfort that can be felt at any given second we reach out and ask. God is there filled with perfect love and perfect reason. I'd be lying if I said every day was bad within my unwanted. Even in the midst of my confusion and fear and my distrust and my blindness, I had laughter. I had added strength to keep going and I had daily assurances. I had profound lessons, which led to God becoming even more *real* to me. Could I trade those lessons? Could I trade my strengthened and real relationship with my God for anything? There's no way. I am not willing to give up the learning and the growing. I am not willing

---

37. Alma 58:11, emphasis added.

to give up the intimate and vulnerable moments because it's those moments that caused my deep trust in Him.

I remember driving home from the gym one day and I was blasting
music just to keep me awake. I felt God. I felt Him. Out of nowhere.
Isn't that wild?! To feel God in unexpected moments like that? Not
in a moment when we are seeking or listening, but when He comes
to us anyway to let us know He's there. Because He knows we really
needed that. I had been struggling in a new season, and I'd been trying
to navigate it and figure it out but was not doing a good job at it. I felt
as though I had been falling and failing, and I felt deflated and heavy.
But then I felt God. And that is enough. Enough to keep going, keep
trying, keep seeking, keep listening, keep trying to figure it out. And I
felt renewed, ya know?

I think in general we have a resistance to things we're not ready
for. We spend time trying, preparing, planning, or waiting, but are
we ever fully ready with what comes our way? I don't know . . . maybe sometimes. It's become a theme in my life that even with my best
efforts of working toward something, God changes my direction or
throws something new into the mix to make me feel that un-readiness.
But I'm getting better at remembering that it is handpicked by God
Himself!

I think we forget that. I think we forget that the unexpected is
God intervening. I think we forget that His whole purpose is to bring
us to the *best* things. I think we forget that we don't truly want things
our way. I think we forget how *thrilling* it is to live by faith. It's all
my unplanned and un-readiness that has really made my relationship
with God personal and real. It's made trusting in Him possible and
desirable. I have really learned to continue to push through the hard,
love the unexpected, and actually look forward to the unwanted. And
what a ride it's been. Take heart in things not going how you wanted,
take heart in your unexpected, in your hard, in your confusing, and
unplanned; it's God *handcrafting* a path that absolutely will be greater
than we ever could have picked, or been ready for, or planned, or prepared for ourselves.

Sometimes our situation won't necessarily change, and sometimes answers aren't there quite yet, but strength is always there. Comfort is always there because God is always there. And He is not overlooking or ignoring or punishing, but in fact, He is working hard with every little detail to be sure things will be *even better* than what we had in mind—all of it part of the plan to begin with, needed and necessary and perfectly crafted for us at every stage and in every season and in every *even worse* moment. Our different and unexpected paths don't take away from the reality that we are in God's hands. Sometimes good things fall apart so better things can fall together. You may not have gone where you had in mind, but you will end up where you needed to be with better blessings. For "he truly spake many great things unto them, which were hard to be understood, save a man should inquire of the Lord."[38]

I know how easy it is to get distracted by a lot of good things to keep us from the best things. I know how badly we want to justify our actions and personal will and pursuits. I know the subtleties from the adversary can be so hard to pick up on sometimes, but I also know His promises are not metaphors or wishful thinking—they're real. And He will show us if we do the new and the scary and the hard

Take time to step back from what makes logical human sense and remember that our God is much greater than all that. Remember His character. Remember the whole existence of the God that is ours is to bring us to the better things. Listen and notice reassurances He gives us that remind us whose hands we're in. Reassurances like the one He gave me when I was telling Him, "This isn't what I wanted," and He compassionately responded, "Why won't you let me bless you?"

Perhaps we can take a step back and be so elated by the fact we have a god on *our* side. A living God here for *you.* That is something to marvel at! That is a reality that should never get belittled. And then we can remember all that we actually *do* have and be profoundly grateful that things never went how we had in mind, because how limiting and lacking would a life that we planned entirely for ourselves be? I really

---

38. 1 Nephi 15:3.

am elated to participate in anything God sees fit, regardless of my narrow-mindedness and personal pursuits. Because even without reaching my *end*, I have found what *truly* sets my soul *dancing*! It's Him.

I hope we don't get caught up in really appealing and realistic snares that chime to our personal vision and become like who Elder Uchtdorf warns members of being, "like passengers on an airplane who spend their time grumbling about the size of the packet of peanuts while they are soaring through the air, far above the clouds—something ancient kings would have given all they possessed to try and experience just once!"[39] Grumbling leads to missing out on what He's bringing to us every day. Narrow vision leads to looking beyond the mark.

I once saw a Lyft driver with all their windows down with just a black lab in the back seat. It made me really happy thinking that dog had important places to be that weekend. Wherever you are and whatever you may be navigating, just remember, God's promises to us are not only fulfilled, but magnified. Looks like I *was* right when I got baptized and I said God was real, and I am His. I may not know the start *and* the end, but I am elated at the cards dealt to me, because those cards came from God's deck and were dealt from God's hands. I don't know how it will work out. I only know that it will. So, gosh dang it, be like that black lab and get out there and *live* knowing that your end *and* your middle and everything in between is in God's hands, and that is *everything*.

"When you let the Lord know that you are serious about doing exactly what you came to earth to do, watch what happens. He may change many things dramatically. So hang on for the ride of your life, the ride that you were born to take."[40]

---

39. "The Joy of the Priesthood," *Ensign*, Nov. 2012.

40. Russell M. Nelson, as quoted in "President Russell M. Nelson Speaks to Millennials about Being Happy," *Church News*, Feb. 23, 2018.

CHAPTER 7

When We Don't
Know What's Right

JOSEPH SMITH WENT WITH HIS QUESTION FOR GOD into the woods about thirty minutes from my house in New York. And how did his answer come? God Himself and Christ our Savior showed up and told him clearly enough that even when death stared him in the face there was still no room for doubt. Lehi and Nephi both saw visions. Joseph in the Old Testament had dreams. Most in the scriptures have angels appear to them. Actually, if I don't think too long on it, most scriptural stories have things happening in big ways, with parted seas and walking on water and burning bushes and mountains moving.

But then there's me over here. And I have never seen a vision or had any breakthrough dreams, and I have never seen God with my human eyes. Wouldn't that have been a cool story to tell you, though? I'm sorry to disappoint and to be a little anticlimactic, but God has never spoken to me in big ways. Which is it not only a little disappointing, because who wouldn't want that? But it can be a little confusing for us trying to figure it all out and do the right thing and stay on His path for us when our answers aren't really coming to us the way we read about it every day in our scriptures.

Asking God can be complicated for us. There are so many different factors and different ways to be mindful of, all topped off with the counsel of "but it's different for everyone," so even other people's advice and experiences can only get us so far sometimes. We go back and forth for so long trying to figure out if it's us or the Spirit. We take chance that the answer is out of our hand because we have to factor in the Lord's timetable. We have to have faith to receive, but also to not counsel our God and not ask for that which is not right. Sometimes it's hard because we feel we cannot hear His answers, and other times things are hard because we do not like the answer we receive. And sometimes through it all we end up standing still trying to make sense of it all because not only is it different for each person, but sometimes it's different for us from the last answer we received. All we want to do is what God wants us to do, but how do we do that when we don't know what that is? Is your head spinning?

The simplest way to start peeling this apart is with a simple question: *is it good?* Once we clearly understand the fruits and characteristics of God and how He communicates, we can more easily discern what is and is not Him. Thinking back on the experience at the weekend girls conference where two thousand girls raised their hands saying they felt the Spirit but then admitted to believing that they have never felt God, I realized the disconnect we have between all the different ways God speaks to us.

I was using this experience for the talk I was going to give the following year at the same youth conference. Before I started my talk, I asked them to write in their journals throughout my talk. I told them not to worry about quoting me or getting things accurate; I wanted them to write whatever it was that came to their minds, especially if it was something I *didn't* say. At the end of my talk, I told them to read their journals to know what God wanted them to know or do or remember or correct. Any time we have ever written down notes from general conference or church or conferences, that is God communicating with us the things He wants you to know. There have actually been more times than I give credit for when, months after general conference, I go back and read my notes I took. Most times I receive counsel and direction I need that I had recorded those months previous. God knew what was coming and what I needed to know and answered me before I even asked.

In contrast, knowing characteristics of God also means understanding the characteristics of Satan. It's crucial to know how the adversary works so we can catch him in his snares and cast him out, and so we can live better without his doubt and weight slowing us down. Things can be complicated without him making it worse. Remember, if something makes you feel bad, negative, or down, that is *not* the Spirit. It's the adversary that stops us or slows us down from growing into the successful, thriving person God intended for us to become all along. Even when our lives need correcting, it is never done in such a way to discourage us, but to build us up and motivate us. When you need to change, pay close attention to your feelings and your thoughts. Do you feel like you're not good enough? Do you feel like you are not worthy to pray and turn to God? Do you feel like all is lost and *why bother?* Is that the God we believe in? Or do we believe in the one who, when we are down and judged by others, like the woman caught in adultery, comes to us on bended knee and says, "Arise, and try again. You have another chance."[41] Knowing the difference between God and the adversary is a game changer. When you turn to Him with a question, pay attention to feelings and thoughts. Because once we realize it's not God, we can exercise our power to cast Satan out and begin to problem solve and move forward without any unnecessary crap complicating it any more.

Let's have this bleed over to acting. How do we know if hard times and fears and doubts are coming from God to stop us from doing what's wrong or from Satan getting in the way to slow us down? When I was supposed to move to Utah, we know that everything fell apart. Too many close calls to things not working out, too many eleventh-hour blessings when the wait made my doubt almost unbearable and family relations worse. Pursuing my move to Utah after baptism caused me to

_____

41. See John 8:11.

do a literal dead-weight belly flop on the ground because of how hard and upsetting everything was. I felt like my answer was to move, but then why was it that the day before I had to be out of my apartment, and after two months of every day looking for a place to live, I still didn't have anything? I had one day before someone else was moving into my apartment, so you can imagine how nervous I was, with me not having anywhere to go. Was all of this happening because it wasn't right? Or was all of this happening because it was, and the adversary was trying to get me to quit?

Oh man was I afraid to move, and I wished so much that I didn't get that answer. But amongst me losing my voice to God over it and every-thing not coming together and being hard and unwanted, moments of reassurance kept coming back. Comfort and calm would come. Amongst it all, good feelings would come. *Good* was there. After marriage, Ben and I wanted to buy a house, so we started looking in Provo. Of course, we'd prayed about it and felt fine, and it made sense for us to do. We met with a realtor, who was awesome and who we saw as a blessing, and off we went for a few weeks looking at homes. But during it all, Ben would have a different recurring idea: *Arizona*. We saw a house we liked, and when we talked about pulling the trigger to make an offer, we just felt . . . *off*. The Spirit speaks to me with recurring thoughts, so we de-cided to pay attention to it and sort it out. We had been praying to find the right house, and we just assumed it would be where we were and reflective of our desires. It took a different perspective for us to realize God was answering our prayers and bringing us to the right house, but it was not where we considered or were seeking out and listening for.

When we are asking for things, what opportunities arise? Could they be related? Is God answering you, but in a different way? It took me years to realize when I was praying and pleading for God to let me serve a mission that He *did*. He brought me to the West, where I became a writer and public speaker. *This is my mission.* This is exact-ly what I asked for, just packaged differently. What if we are getting answers to our prayers, but we don't recognize them because we are too intent on getting a specific answer to match our specific vision? Sometimes we don't recognize our answers because we are blinded by wanting confirmation of our own desires and we fail to see that the Lord would have us do something else.

Let's finally go full circle on this unemployment experience. I've been saving this for this exact section. You'll never guess what I did when that better job with *better* pay finally came. I declined it. A call came with a job I didn't even apply to, and *wow* were the blessings attached to his job extensive. But we weren't looking for work in Utah; we were looking in Arizona. And we all know I didn't want to leave. I turned to Ben, and I said, "I know this is a huge opportunity. I know that taking this job will end the longest trial that we've just barely survived, and I know this will put an end to our pleadings and fasts, but I don't want it." Ugh, I sound like the worst when I type it like this. How dumb could I be, right? But it was so important to me to stay in Arizona that I was willing to struggle longer for it.

Yes or no questions are tricky in prayers. We can easily and unconsciously stay standing with no progress for a long time trying to detect if it was a yes or no that we're getting in return. Am I only hearing yes because it's what I want to hear? Is it me or the Spirit? And then we go back and forth and back and forth, and then we end up just stuck. Well, I didn't have time to be stuck. I needed to tell them the next morning if I was going to take the job or not. I knew I didn't want to exclude God completely from this, but I also knew I didn't have time to go back and forth and back on *wait, was that me because I don't want it, or was that the Spirit?* So, I just picked. And I decided I was going to struggle longer for what I wanted. Ben—he's so good—responded with, "I trust you."

Before hopping in bed, I told God, "Thank you. Thank you for this. It shows me that you are there, and that is a blessing. I'm not going to take it. If that is wrong, let me know before 8 a.m., when I have to send them the email with my response." And that was that. I fell asleep. I learned the biggest prayer hack of my existence. It, *so far,* has a 100 percent success rate: God doesn't always tell us what is right, but He will *always* tell us what is wrong. It's a promise to us that He will *not* lead us astray. He will tell us in discomfort and feeling *off.* Or in this case, I woke up at four in the morning and I shot up in bed wide awake from a deep sleep and knew immediately that I had made the wrong decision. I ended up sending my acceptance email right then at four in the morning.

Sometimes we just need to pick and move forward. Sometimes the worst thing we can do is simply stay in the same spot making no progress—that's Satan's way. Sometimes the fastest way to progress and move onward and upward is to just pick and move forward and see what falls in or out of our lives. Like the popular Mormon Message with Elder Holland about the wrong roads, where a man and his son both felt they should go one way when they reached a fork in the road, only to find out it was a dead end—so then they corrected course and knew they were steadily going in the right direction.[42] Even if we do choose a *wrong path*, He will always tell us, and then we can more quickly correct course and move forward, onward and upward.

I think of the analogy of the man on the side of the road with a busted car. Who will God help faster? Someone who is praying and pleading for help? Or someone who says a prayer and then opens the hood and starts tinkering? Probably the second one. Because the second one is moving and working and making it easier for God to help him. How can He move us in the right direction if we aren't in motion? He can, but that version is the longer version.

Sometimes He asks us to do the problem solving and bring our solution to Him. I think of Ether 2, when the brother of Jared had to figure out what they were going to do so that they wouldn't spend 344 days on the water in complete darkness. He didn't postpone his original answer to build the barges. He didn't sit still, waiting for an answer to fall in his lap. He kept moving forward and gave God something to work with. It was the brother of Jared who came up with the stone idea, and Heavenly Father magnified it and off they went![43] I think of Nephi when his and his brother's bows broke. Laman and Lemuel took the slow approach and retreated in their efforts. They talked and complained and thought a lot about their situation and how unwanted

---

42. "Wrong Roads," Gospel Media Library.
43. See Ether 2, 3.

it was. Nephi on the other hand, kept moving. Maybe he knew that it is easier for God to redirect us if we are already in motion. Nephi problem solved with a sling and stones, brought that to the Lord and inquired of Him, and then God directed his course and Nephi slayed wild beasts. When he returned, Laman and Lemuel had made no progress, and there they were, standing still.[44]

Are we moving forward and bringing *something* to the Lord? Or are we still on the side of the road with a broken car, hoping someone else will drive by with a solution?

When we were moving from New York to Arizona, it was my fifth time driving across the country. I know this is a bucket-list item for a lot of people, but I was happy to never do it again after the first time. We did the driving days in twelve-hour increments—drive twelve hours, sleep at a hotel. Another twelve hours the next day, sleep at a hotel. It was a total of forty-three hours driving, I was in one car with a pregnancy bladder and our two kids. Ben was in our other car with our two giant, hundred-pound dogs. We were caught in tornadoes our first two days driving through the East Coast. I've driven through some crazy torrential downpours before, but torrential is not tornado. I found out there is most definitely a difference. We were driving three miles an hour, mostly just idling forward. Ben was in front of me, and I could not see him. We couldn't see any cars around us. We couldn't see lines, couldn't see flashing lights—we could only hear the rain, which sounded like it was going to dent our hood and sirens. I was worried I would only know where a car was once I heard the crunch of me hitting one, or one hitting me. My Fitbit kept vibrating, saying I was "stressed" and needed to take some deep breaths to calm my heart rate—haha! This was a very long car ride, and it was most definitely longer than the twelve hours we had planned for.

We made it to the hotel. Eventually. We clicked through all the news channels on TV, and every station was talking about the tornado we had just driven through and how bad it was. We anxiously awaited the fate of tomorrow's weather when we would do another twelve-hour

---

44. See 1 Nephi 16.

shift of driving to where our next hotel was already booked. More tornados. We thought and prayed long and hard about what we were going to do. *Do we drive? Do we stay in Indiana?* We decided to drive. We consciously made the decision to do the scariest drive of our lives all over again. But if we would have stayed, thinking it was safer or the best idea, we would have been in tornado storms for almost a whole week. Instead we drove through, and it was only two hours. What if standing still, thinking we're safe, is actually causing more harm or damage or delays? Are we moving forward, continuously making progress, or are we staying stagnant, causing lingering and unnecessary storms for ourselves? Causing postponed progress and blessings?

But what if we don't understand why God would want us to do something He's asked of us? It happens frequently for me. Our redirection can seem a little confusing or unrelated at first. But *isn't it a thrill?* I think again of Nephi when he says, "The Lord hath commanded me to make these plates for a wise purpose in him, which purpose I know not."[45] Or Moroni, who simply was acting on what could be recurring thoughts like we talked about: "And I do this for a wise purpose; for thus it whispereth me, according to the workings of the Spirit of the Lord which is in me. And now, I do not know all things; but the Lord knoweth all things which are to come; wherefore, he worketh in me to do according to his will."[46] Or really, it can make us think of a lot of the prophets who contributed to scriptures but may not have fully known why. Well jeez, what if their lack of understanding had stopped them from pursuing? So if you're confused about what you're working toward, you're in good company. And here we are with the Book of Mormon! *"But the Lord knoweth all things from the beginning."*[47]

I like picturing our *whisperings* and our recurring thoughts as second chances. Just in case the first time it came we might have dismissed it as a fleeting or weird thought. Or maybe we didn't pay attention because it was a new or different thought that would lead us in a different direction than our intended desire? I like to picture our third

---

45. 1 Nephi 9:5.
46. Words of Mormon 1:7.
47. 1 Nephi 9:6.

or fourth chance to try again to heed it as reassurance that it wasn't a fluke and we need to pay attention and start taking them more seriously. I don't know, I've always just liked to picture our whisperings and our recurring thoughts as our souls directing and guiding and pulling us to what we were meant to do all along. As if our souls remember more than we do. I received a priesthood blessing once in which I was told to *pay close attention to that spiritual being living within you.* A reality we really should start taking more seriously.

When I got in my car accident and had a bad neck injury and arms I couldn't move for a week, I had a fireside that next day. You should know that I am *very* good at saying no. Almost too good at saying no. But that's not what this is about. It's about discerning what God wants us to do for that biggest purpose we may not understand. That following day after my accident I got a priesthood blessing that told me that *some things He requires of me and He will help me with, but others are not necessary.* That morning I was supposed to have a book signing. It was something that was well promoted for so long with a *lot* of people attending. Though I hated to do so at the last second, with no chance to get the word out to others, I canceled. I felt that this was something that just wasn't *needed.* I did, however, feel that fireside *did* need to happen for that wise purpose in Him, and I knew He was going to sustain me and help me make it through because it's what He was requiring of me at the time. And He did. And I'm hopeful that something I said was used as a tool to help others God knew would be in attendance.

A few months later, I was in the emergency room for the entire night. I needed my gallbladder out. Now, I know if there were a worthy and justified reason to ever cancel last minute on anything, surgery was the reason. And I had a plane ticket to California that next morning. *Is this something I can cancel, or do I keep going and He will sustain me?* But even though they were telling me I needed it out and could be taken back right then, *oh* I just felt this pull. Not guilt or obligation, but a *pull* from my, well, I'll call it *gut* for now, saying I needed to go. I might have made a face or something, but Ben looked at me and just knew I was not going into surgery in that moment. He must be used to me doing things that don't seem logical, but the doctors were not used to it at all. They clearly thought I was crazy, *but* they did say I could go as long as I was on medication. So I went from the ER to the airport, flew to California on strong pain medications, spoke, flew home, went right back to the hospital, and had surgery.

When I was walking on the stand, I saw a familiar face that I thought I was hallucinating, maybe from the meds they gave me, because it didn't make any sense to me. The classic story of me meeting the missionaries is well known by this point because it's a little ridiculous. When I met the elders just from us being on a sidewalk at the same time as each other, I told them I would only listen if they brought me a steak to eat. I didn't think they'd actually do it. I thought it was a clever way to get rid of them. But they did. That's how it all got started. And as I was walking on the stand, I *thought* I saw the missionary who brought me the steak. But I was in California, and he does *not* live in California. Turns out, it was him! *Oh*, how wild it was to see him again for the first time in years and years! The stake that asked me to come out also flew him out as a surprise for me, and I had no idea! He got up and introduced me and shared the most beautiful stories and experiences and feelings that left me almost immobile because in that moment I knew that although nothing made logical sense at first, I needed to be there. I knew that it was profoundly right. And *wow* what I would have missed out on if I hadn't taken the time to inquire and converse with God about it. What have I previously missed out on because I dismissed it as crazy or illogical?

When I was confirmed a member of the Church, it blew getting baptized out of the water. When I got baptized, I was happy because I knew what I had done, but mostly I was wet. And cold. But when I got the gift of the Holy Ghost, that was a *physical* thing for me. I *physically* felt myself get that gift. The contrast really was huge. After going twenty-one years without it, the difference really was *real*. But what of those who got confirmed at eight? Or just younger in their life in general? What of those who don't have that contrast? Does it make the promise of the Spirit always being with us less true? Or are we so used to working with it for so long, we don't give it full credit? What if it's guiding and speaking and directing us so seamlessly because of the promise of it always being with us, that we don't even know what it's like to not have it? We overlook it and take it for granted because it's ingrained so well in us, just like He promised. Most times it's so subtle we don't recognize it at all, and we attribute it to us just being us and acting without thought and out of personality or character. Sometimes, and more commonly, we attribute the more noticeable feelings to being our *gut* feelings. As we see these new ideas and different opportunities and our recurring thoughts, instead of wondering, what if we took confidence in being a confirmed member and moved forward knowing that if it were wrong God would let us know? How would life blossom if we stripped down some layers of second guessing and standing still and took confidence in the resources and promises He has given us?

Well, what if our answer is that our answer isn't coming yet? I think of all the battles in Alma. Sometimes they were directed to *act* and fight. And sometimes they were directed to wait. But in both cases, they were counseled to be *faithful*. So how can we move forward if our answer is to wait? By staying faithful and hopeful in Him regardless.

Well, what if we are given more than one option that seems like a good idea? This was a hang-up for Ben and me for a while. While in Arizona at the start of unemployment, we lived in a little city called Coolidge. And when I say little, I mean the only thing out there was a Family Dollar and cotton fields. Phoenix was an hour one way, and Tucson was an hour the other. We were going back and forth about if we should invest in moving to Tucson in hopes of having better chances for work. Ben got a blessing that said it didn't matter what we chose. That bugged us. How could it not matter? Did it not matter because God did not care? Was our unemployment not important enough to God? Why couldn't He just tell us? At the time, that counsel seemed to not help, so we moved to Tucson anyway. But then it clicked. When we took that job that would bring us back to Utah, we then saw that us moving to Tucson or staying in Coolidge really didn't matter after all because God knew it wasn't going to keep us from where we *needed* to be next. Sometimes there will be things that won't really matter because our decisions won't take us away from promised blessings and needed experiences. Sometimes He wants us to make the decisions ourselves. Sometimes what's most important is making sure we're practicing agency, because if He were to tell us every little move and answer for us, it would make everything we fought for against Satan and his plan to go *down* in vain.

"The truth is that sometimes it just doesn't matter to the Lord what you decide, as long as you stay within the fundamental covenants and principles of the gospel. . . .

"Your work is to make the best decisions you can based on the information available to you, grounded in the values and principles of the gospel. Then strive with all your might to succeed in the things you undertake—and be faithful.

"Do that and the dots will connect.

"Perhaps it's disappointing to hear that God won't necessarily give you a detailed itinerary for your life's journey. But do you really want direction in every detail of your life?

"Do you really want someone giving you the cheat codes to life before you have a chance to figure things out for yourself? What kind of adventure would that be?

"My dear young friends, you pass through the adventure of mortality only once. Wouldn't an individually tailored walkthrough complete with spoilers and answers to all of life's great questions take away your great feeling of accomplishment and your increase of confidence in the Lord and in yourself?

"Because God has given you agency, there are many directions you can choose to go and still lead a fulfilling life. Mortality is actually an open-ended, choose-your-own-adventure story. You have commandments, you have covenants, you have inspired prophetic counsel, and you have the gift of the Holy Ghost. That is more than enough to lead you to mortal happiness and eternal joy. Beyond that, don't despair if you make some decisions that are less than perfect. That is how you learn. That's part of the adventure!

"No, adventures never go smoothly from start to finish, but if you're faithful, you can be assured of a happy ending."[48]

Well, what if we are overwhelmed with all the repeated verses in the scriptures saying all we have to do is *ask*, and if it is right, He will grant it to us, but we don't know if what we're asking for is right? How can we act according to the Spirit if we don't know if what we are doing is of the Spirit or not? Sometimes I get frustrated trying to sort out the right thing because I know if we ask, we shall receive *if* it is right, but I don't know what right is. I just want to do what God wants me to, but sometimes I don't know what that is! What if we asked for help? What if it really is as simple as asking Him, but what if it's asking Him for help to know what to ask for? A hack I love and learned out of desperation was to start my prayer with, *"Heavenly Father, help me with this prayer."* I had gotten so drained from not knowing what to do that I didn't even know how to pray for that situation anymore. And what happened? The coolest thing happened, that's what. In that prayer, I asked for things I had *never* thought of before until I said them out loud in the prayer. He really actually *told* me in the moment as I was praying because I asked for help with my prayer. Maybe I shouldn't be surprised by this. Maybe it shouldn't be surprising to us that God is not playing a weird guessing game with us. It's not a game at all; it's us just learning and experiencing His vastness, and I think it's a *thrill* to continue to see God work in His many ways.

Just like all of us, I, too, have fallen victim to the snares of doubt. I, too, have fallen victim to confusion. Fallen victim to blindness because I am so passionate about my narrow mindedness. To distraction. To logic. Fallen victim to keeping God at arm's length. Fallen victim to yelling at God, wondering where He is and why isn't He there with me. But then I remember something.

God.

48. Dieter F. Uchtdorf, "The Adventure of Mortality," Worldwide Devotional for Young Adults, Jan. 14, 2018.

I remember who God truly is and His promises. I remember His whole purpose is to be there for us and to help us succeed. I remember His vastness and find it a thrill to allow life to blossom the way He would have it. We have a God who is oh so *good*. His promises and dedication are *real*. He is real. He's as real as your heart beating this exact second. And this exact second, God is mindful of you. And the second after that. And all the seconds after that.

Your prayers *have* been heard, but *greater* is what He has in store for you.

CHAPTER 8

When We Want to Give Up

CHICAGO O'HARE AIRPORT is the worst airport for delays. Actually, it is award-winning for being the second-worst airport in the entire U.S. for delays and cancelations. And lucky for me, every single one of my flights from Rochester, New York, stops in Chicago to connect me to wherever I'm going to speak. It's embarrassing how well I know that airport. I know what bathrooms in what terminal never have lines, and I know what stalls have broken hooks so you can't hang your purse up. Not something I like to publicly brag about. I have a very short list of things I *really* dislike, but the Chicago airport, I'm certain, is at the top. That place has caused me so much grief. I went almost nine months straight with *every single* speaking engagement I was flying for being delayed or canceled—it's still ridiculous to me.

After taking two months off for the holidays, I was back to traveling two weekends out of the month, which means I was back at that airport a lot again. Every time I would go from Rochester to Chicago for my layover it was as if I braced myself for impact of something bad happening because it has so frequently before. Just walking around, I can think of so many experiences of misery there in great detail. I walk by a Manchu Wok and can think of two times I was given a food voucher for delayed flights due to bad weather and that's where I went to eat. I walk by the second bench on my right in a tunnel of windows leading to the furthest gates away for the smaller planes, and I remember a time I was crying on it after being told I wouldn't make it home for another day. I go into Jamba Juice and employees say, "Back again?" So here I was, back at it again, leaving my fate in the hands of Chicago O'Hare, and immediately before unbuckling my seat I had all these negative thoughts come to me. But then . . . nothing happened. I was tense and negative out of habit, but then I made my connection out of there and on the flights returning home with ease.

I wonder how many times I subconsciously do that with other aspects of my life? Have you ever gotten to a point where you expect bad things to happen because they have in the past? When I sat on my next plane confused about why things worked out, I realized how we can unintentionally limit and trap ourselves from allowing things to be different because we have been hurt in the past.

I think of this video of a man and a woman riding on an escalator when it all of a sudden stops and breaks. One says, frustrated, "I don't believe this," while the other one starts yelling for help, "Hello? Anyone there? If you can hear me, there are two people stuck on the escalator!" That's right, an escalator. When I show this video to others, everyone always laughs because they aren't really stuck. But it does pose valid questions we all need to ask ourselves at some point: *Are we really stuck?* Are we the ones getting in our own way?

When I think of the times I feel stuck, I'm learning to question me before I question God. *Am I selling myself short and limiting myself? Is my perspective skewed and limited due to my own blindness from trying to protect myself from getting burned again?*

Are we seeing the start of something as negative before anything happens? Are we letting past experiences or feelings hinder new ones? Hinder a chance at redemption and good things? Are we so upset or distracted or caught up in another vision for ourselves that we don't realize that our escalator becomes stairs? Are we beginning to believe things can't be different? Are we realizing and taking advantage of other things that we have to keep us moving forward?

Are we like those in Mormon who "did struggle for their lives without calling upon that Being who created them"?[49] Are we taking advantage of everything we have? Are we taking advantage of the resources we have been taught and given? Are we really honestly doing the simple things of the gospel? The times I have taken a step back to think about what I have or have not been doing, it's pretty common I find that *I'm* the one who hasn't kept my end of the agreement, not God. Are some of our challenges harder because of our lack of efforts or narrowed vision?

It's easy to think we know better when we observe things with our mortal eyes and with the knowledge we have been given. We ask God why He is doing something a certain way with us and our situations when things don't seem to add up for us. Like in Jacob, when the laborer asks, "Why are you bringing that branch to the poorest soil?" And we ask, "Why are you bringing me to this unwanted spot? What good could come from this?" But the next time we look around and things look dark and it seems we are working against the odds and logic, and we wonder how anyone could grow under those circumstances, think of the olive trees. Little growth and a lot of correction comes to those who are in a desired place or a place of comfort, and the much growth and the much fruit came from those in the less-than-ideal spot.

What if Peter sinking as he tried walking on the water wasn't just about doubt? What if there's more to it that causes him to sink? When watching the Bible video of this, I love watching Peter right before he sinks. Wind comes and thunder cracks, and he starts looking around at his surroundings, then he loses focus and becomes distracted.[50] Distracted from what he's doing and distracted from Christ. Distracted by things we feel are worthy variables, when in fact, they aren't. What if, like the laborer in the vineyard, we look around and become distracted by what doesn't make sense and spend our time worrying about things that really only end up taking our focus off Christ and His ability to do the impossible and defy logical odds?

49. Mormon 5:2.
50. "Wherefore Didst Thou Doubt?" *The Life of Jesus Christ Bible Videos*, ChurchofJesusChrist.org/bible-videos.

Are we trapping ourselves? Are we getting too distracted by all these other variables that we lose focus on the most important? Are we missing things to do or opportunities coming up or resources available to see our escalator as stairs?

But what of the times we are doing everything we can and we have nothing to show for our efforts? What if we are trying so *hard* that we feel we have depleted any and all possibilities to help our situations and to help ourselves?

One of the first scriptures I just happened to ever memorize was 3 Nephi 13:33: "But seek ye first the kingdom of God and his righteousness, and all these things shall be added unto you." But I guess I didn't know that it would be what sometimes was the only thing I had left to cling to. I held on to supposed promise while everything was pulling me full force by my ankles, and I held on to that scripture with my fingertips, hoping that my losses really would be made up if I put God first. There have been times when I didn't have energy left, times when I didn't have any strength left, times when I felt I had to force myself to use this faith when I didn't even know if I had faith left. But I held on to this pre-baptism scripture, hoping this was true and really would come to pass, because I had too many times when I felt like my losses were too much to continue. Because I had too many times when I felt like there was nothing else I could do that I wasn't already doing. On my infamous move from New York to Utah, things were not working out and time was passing by, and I had nothing to show for my efforts. The weight seemed too heavy, the end didn't seem close, it seemed it was one thing after another, and my body ached at the thought of going on with little change. I was *exhausted*. I just physically ached from everything I was putting in, and I was mad at seeing nothing come out. I was mad—I was mad at God. I was yelling at Him, saying, "I don't know what else to do! I'm praying, I'm reading, I'm fasting, I don't know how many times!" I had dedicated all of my free time into looking and planning and researching. I had sacrificed so much. "Do you even care still? Do you even care about me?" I felt stuck and I wasn't seeing any stairs. What if my only option left was to give up?

I was lying on the floor after yelling at God, and my eyes were closed, not necessarily because I was praying but because I was too exhausted and too afraid to open them. And I was just lying on the floor for a little bit, when then I saw Christ. I was lying on the floor with my eyes closed, and I saw Christ standing right in front of me. Can you picture that? Picture for a minute what He looks like to you. And then, He smiles. He smiles *at you*.

"Cast your mind upon the night that you cried unto me in your heart, that you might know concerning the truth of these things. Did I not speak peace to your mind concerning the matter? What greater witness can you have than from God?"[51] That was it. It's all I needed. To know no matter how much was difficult, no matter how much I didn't understand, and no matter what I was doing, He was happy with me. That it was right.

"Yes, there are cautions and considerations to make, but once there has been genuine illumination, beware the temptation to retreat from a good thing. If it was right when you prayed about it and trusted it and lived for it, it is right now. Don't give up when the pressure mounts. . . . Don't give in. Certainly don't give in to that being who is bent on the destruction of your happiness. He wants everyone to be miserable like unto himself. Face your doubts. Master your fears. 'Cast not away therefore your confidence.' Stay the course and see the beauty of life unfold for you."[52]

Things may seem dark right now, things may seem never ending right now, but in those moments, I think of a priesthood blessing I once received that quite literally changed me. It's changed how I think and how I act, and it's been something I think of often in these times when we feel we don't see an end or when we want to give up. It's shaped my view on the reality of perspective.

It was the week of my second child's due date, and the priesthood blessings that I received just so happened to mention our

---

51. D&C 6:22–23.
52. Jeffrey R. Holland, "'Cast Not Away Therefore Your Confidence,'" BYU Speeches, Mar. 2, 1999.

soon-to-be-born son. I was told that he and Gracie picked me to be their mom. I was told that he's watched over me throughout my life. I was told that he misses Ben and I and is very anxious to be reunited with us, and especially to be back with Gracie. He and Gracie were inseparable before she was born. I was told that Gracie would recognize him when she sees him.

Goose bumps.

Often when we think of families, we think of the here and the hereafter. It's not often we stop and think that we were all united together already *before* here. And this has nothing to do with giving birth, but overall, whether in reference to your parents and siblings, those that you adopt or foster, members of the Church or not, alive or not yet or no longer, etc. It doesn't necessarily matter how our families are brought together here on earth, but that we existed and interacted and loved *beforehand.* And now, with them watching over and helping us here. Interacting, learning, growing, and loving. Each unique. Each necessary for experiences and lessons intertwined between us that are too intricate to fully understand, to reconnect us from *before*, to help us grow *here*, and to prepare us for the *hereafter.*

Perhaps reading this you can recall too many times to count when you have felt that deep and eternal connection to those in your family on the other side of the veil and feel their influence on you, some during little everyday things, and some through sacred and personal experiences or blessings. So, what's my point? My point is that we are not alone. Not only is God absolutely always, at all times mindful of us, but He has blessed us with those on both sides of the veil as well, watching over and cheering for us. Unseen *protection* and guidance from those anxious to be born, and from those already passed.

My point is that we are sometimes in need of a reality check, especially in those dark times when we feel we may be stuck forever. We should be doing more than just existing and more than just *getting by.* Let's refocus, often, on who we truly are and what we are a part of. Refocus on the reality of being a living soul that can never die. We have forever built into our genes. Who we are and what we're a part of has real meaning, deep roots that extend far beyond this sphere and most definitely far beyond our current challenges. Roots that should drive our priorities and affect what we do daily with our lives. Which means our suffering now is temporary.

My point is that our perspective and how we see things matters. How we spend our time matters. My point is this is not the start of me and my soon-to-be son. *This life is not the start of you.* Because *here* isn't everything; there is so much more to come, in this life *and* so much hereafter. This is not the beginning, and this is not the end. We are all without beginnings. We have qualities and traits of divinity, created by and passed to us from the most powerful being to ever exist.

Things may seem dark right now, things may seem never-ending right now, and giving up may seem like the only option left, but it's not. Because eternity is reality. Because we are part of something *so* much bigger than the here and the now.

When a baby is born and the parents hold them for the first time, they look down at them and are just so overwhelmingly consumed with *love* for their baby. And it wasn't because the baby did anything— it couldn't; it was just born. It's not that the baby accomplished anything to earn that love. The parents profoundly and deeply loved that child simply because it was *theirs*. When I think of the times when I have doubts and I complain and I fail and fall, sometimes I wonder *why* the Lord would ever want to be yoked with someone like *me*. But He reminds me that I don't need to earn anything from Him, but simply and profoundly because *I'm His*. How much does He love us? Even as much as He hath "graven thee upon the palms of [His] hands."[53]

Like in Ether, sometimes we feel we are crossing great storms buried in the sea in darkness, but the light we do have, even if it may seem as small as a stone, will be what we need to make it through. And it's just not making it through this lifetime, because it's not ever about just making it to the end and hoping for a better go at it in the next round, the hereafter. Because like in Ether, life didn't end for them when they reached land. It wasn't *the end* to the story or to them. They continued

---

53. Isaiah 49:16.

living and they enjoyed new seasons with blessings and prosperity. So no, it's not just about trying to get by until we die. It's about holding on to the light we *do* have, knowing a new season *will* come in *this* life, one filled with blessings and prosperity.

The woman who had a blood disease struggled most of her life. She used every resource and penny she had to find relief and progress and healing, but it just never happened. I know she felt loss of hope, loss of strength, and loss of faith, and she probably thought often about how maybe she's the exception to life getting better *here*. We don't know who she is—she's not named in the scriptures—but how much we can relate to her. To those times, those unanswered prayers, unfulfilled fasts, passing time, unwanted and uncharted paths. Times when it seems things have gotten worse from doing what we think is right. Times when it seems we're out of sight or lost from God. A stranger. Alone. Unnamed or unimportant. "Who am I? What if I'm the exception?" we ask.

Those feelings are a heavy weight. But although the effects of feeling those things are real, being hidden and out of sight from God is not. Though those feelings can be real to us, we will always be worthy of His love and attention. How? Well because we are His. And that makes us enough. That. is. everything.

So how can an all-knowing, all-powerful God also be personal? Because our God is a "one by one" God. Personal and individual. Because like Christ, who was walking in streets that were so busy, it was like sardines, shoulder-to-shoulder foot traffic, and Christ stopped and asked, "*Who touched me?*"[54] His disciples were probably confused by such an odd question because everyone was touching them. But like God, our Savior is a "one by one" Savior. One who notices us on the ground buried under the crowd.

Like the woman at the well, our "one by one" God travels the long way on purpose and comes to us. Like the woman with the blood disease on the street grabbing his clothes in the shoulder-to-shoulder

---

54. Luke 8:45.

crowd, our "one by one" Savior notices us and stops for us and heals us. And although they are unnamed in the scriptures, He knows them.

When we feel like He has turned His back on us, we only need to turn around. Because although we may feel alone or forgotten, He knows us. Exactly and perfectly does He know what we're going through and know what we're feeling. He knows all of you because He created all of you with His hands.[55] And we too can overcome thoughts from the adversary by knowing and saying what Christ said, "And yet I am not alone, because the Father is with me."[56] We will always be enough. And if we hold on and allow God to be God, we will see Him come to us, and like the scripture I first memorized, our losses *will be made up* and we'll receive our promised blessings. All the promises, all the blessings we're trying *so hard* to attain, in scriptures, they're all written in past-tense, *prepared.* They're already there. Heavenly Father has *already* spent the time, the work, the effort into preparing the best ever created. And we can have it if we just keep going.

We have times when we feel like the stripling warriors, who were asked to fight what seemed was a losing battle against an enemy that was innumerable. We all have times when we feel like David, who had to *fight alone* against a *champion.* But David *did* in fact kill the infamous giant Goliath. And the sons of Helaman came out winning without losing a *single* soul.

Are we going to be mad there's a battle? Are we going to *allow* the adversary to tell us all is lost? Or that the odds aren't in our favor? Or that we aren't deserving? Are we going to stay stuck? Or are we going to fight knowing *who* is with us and see the miracles? And from what I have learned over and over again, after twenty years of doing it myself, and ten years sacrificing and struggling with God, truly the greatest things do come only from Him, the giver of all good gifts. "When I can't see the hand of God, I should trust his heart. I know what kind of heart he has."[57]

---

55. See Alma 18:32.
56. John 16:32.
57. David Butler, *Almighty: How the Most Powerful Being in the Universe Is Also Your Loving Heavenly Father* (Deseret Book, 2018).

When I feel the weight of my situations get really heavy, and I feel I can no longer handle the weight, I desperately need the helping hand of the Savior. A hand that is never shortened. A hand that is always extended. A loving and understanding and an always-there hand. A capable and indestructible hand. An all-powerful, perfect hand. When I feel momentarily buried and burned out from my efforts and situation, I'm learning to better grab for that hand. And the cool thing is that every time we make efforts to reach for it, a literal Savior comes to our aid and saves us, bears our burdens, lightens our loads. Strengthens. Comforts. Renews. Revives. Carries.

So yeah, sometimes we feel like we are struggling and gasping and sinking, sometimes we feel dizzy from the too-quick change of course, sometimes we feel our strength has run so thin that another day doesn't seem like another chance, but another burden to bear—but, like Peter on the water, He will not let us drown. He will pull us up. He will save us. Every day. A million times a day, if we need. If we but reach. That's a reality.

When we are praying and when we are trying, and things don't work out, rest assured it will always be His will. And it will, in fact, always be better. And you know what? Comfort is always there because Christ is always there. And you know what? The future holds everything for us. Life truly is a *thrill*, even with the ugly-cry moments.

Remembering whose hands we're in is what makes those ugly-cry moments, those weak, disheartening, and heavy moments, an intimate moment with a perfect Savior. And knowing who's on our side and who's *by* our side absolutely gives me reason to keep going, keep trying, keep smiling, keep turning to Him, and to look forward with hope and joy for another day. Another moment.

Because even in hard times, life is *oh so* good. Because whether in hard times or not, we are never alone. We will not drown. We are His, and that is *everything*. We have the *most* powerful, all-knowing Being to ever exist on *our* side. And hard times may always be there, but so will God.

So yeah, maybe things are really hard right now. And yeah, maybe we wish things were going differently. But you know what? God is real. And He is there. And you know what? Motivation and comfort and guidance and energy and a new mindset are a prayer away. And you know what? The future holds *everything* for us.

And the cool thing is, because of God, *every passing second* is a chance to turn it all around! So cheers! Cheers to endless do-overs! Cheers to endless comfort! Cheers to endless love, and endless guidance, and endless strength, and endless forgiveness.

Because our trials and our changes of course will never alter the unchanging truth that God is real and is leading us to the best blessings. Because we have a God with endless resources on our side, and how empowering is that?! That absolutely gives me every reason to choose laughter. And choose faith. And choose to smile, every day. To me, He is every reason to be happy and to make even the hard days not as hard. Trust God with your life—after all, He's the one who gave it to you.

CHAPTER 9

When We Don't Fit In

IT WAS THE DEAD OF SUMMER, just two degrees short of one hundred, and I couldn't put off going to the store anymore. I was standing in the mirror looking at myself, sweating. And as the sweat dewed on my arm, I pulled a thick nude stocking all the way up my arm until it reached my shoulder and adjusted it so it stopped at my wrist. It was like what burn victims would wear, and mine was extra thick so it wouldn't keep sliding down. I hated that thing. But I hated the stares even more. I wiped the sweat off my forehead and took another look in the mirror before taking a huge breath and bearing the trip to the store. How did I get to this point in my life?

At the age of twenty-one, for the first time in my life I was struggling with something so foreign to me: discomfort with myself. There is so much diversity in New York, where I'm from, that we don't do double takes, even with the most bizarre things. And then I moved. And here I was, unrealistically covering my arms like a burn victim to cover up tattoos because I just couldn't handle the comments. I just hadn't figured out how to handle the stares and the judgments and the silence and the parents pulling their kids in closer to them when I'd walk by. I had just sacrificed my relationships with my family and the only way of living I knew to follow God across the country to a place I had never been before, not knowing a single person, and cannonballed into being treated as if I were the modern-day Korihor.

And with passing time, it was all I could notice. And with passing time and not figuring out how to handle any of this yet, I started to crumble. I stayed in the house when I didn't want to just because I just didn't want to be around any of that. Now if you've read my first book, then you know the in-depth story of all this. And then when we fast-forward to now, with me doing what I'm doing and accomplishing what I have, it's a funny thing.

I don't fit the mold for anything. I don't fit the mold of how I look in my religion, my community, and what I'm trying to tackle and talk about and pursue. How can someone succeed when everything about them in their demographic implies that they shouldn't? It's like I was failing before I could even start. Sometimes fears are in our head and we imagine the worst-case scenario, and that's enough to stop before starting. But not in my case—mine was a reality. I couldn't go anywhere or post anything without those terrible stares, mean comments, rude remarks, assumptions of my hatred toward the gospel and toward God, emails saying I should end my life or that God could never love someone like me. Silence from guys my age because surely I wasn't temple worthy and it was best just to steer clear. It was a long time of loneliness and heartache and weight and judging and confusion and anger toward others, myself, and also toward God. *How could they act like this? Maybe they're right and I'm flawed and just not good enough. How could God even allow this to happen?*

And, you know, it was much deeper than just my appearance. Nothing about me is "typical" in my religion's demographic, although I'm not really sure what that means anyway. I don't know how to cook. I can't play piano and sew my own dresses. I "have a past" with no family roots in the gospel. I never wanted to be a mom until I became one. And once I did, I was the one who worked full-time and my husband was home with the kids while he did school full-time online because that was the season we were in. It seems as though I will always be in a season of atypical, no matter what shape that takes. But I have learned to really run with it.

It was a brutally lonely and long process. But I got tired, ya know? I just got so tired of being upset and feeling down and being mad and being hurt and not liking myself. That's not who I was. I missed me. I got tired of second-guessing and closing up and being everything I wasn't. And for what? People I would never see again? I decided to worry about me and worry about what God wanted me to be doing and working toward and worry about my recurring thoughts. Because our crazy, wonderful recurring thoughts are how our soul speaks to us to reach what we were meant to do all along! The best ways we can make progress and thrive is to pay close attention to our souls, those spiritual beings living within us. It's smarter and more powerful than most any other force, if we but take a chance.

It was a lot of prayer. A lot of pleading to God. A lot of long stares in the mirror. A lot of pushing my comfort levels and a whole lot of tearing down to undo and rebuild. It was a lot of honest conversations with my Creator. I really desperately needed to see myself, to see even a sliver of how God saw me, because I wasn't seeing it. I was seeing my setbacks and my differences and everything I wish was different about me and everything that would blossom in my life if I could make those changes. And that took asking Him to show me that and, yeah, longer looks in the mirror until I saw it. Uncomfortable, but life changing.

Turning to God and being productive with Him took a lot of effort, but I am confident that what I have learned can never undo the confidence and knowledge I have built up in myself and who I am.

Interesting, isn't it?

Because of Isaiah's prophecy, for centuries, many young Jewish women had dreamed and wondered, "Will I be chosen as the mother of the Messiah?" But not Mary. When she was told she was going to be the mother of Christ, she tried to tell the angel that it shouldn't be her. She saw herself as a handmaid" In Hebrew, "handmaid" translates to "slave."

Interesting, isn't it? How we are so quick to do that to ourselves. How we are so quick to see ourselves as less. How it is so unconsciously easy for us to sometimes deny ourselves of things because we don't think we are worthy of them. Or capable of them. Or surely someone else would be a better fit than us—for reasons too numerable to list.

Not necessarily saying that Mary did this, but interesting, isn't it? How hard it is to gap together how we see ourselves versus how God sees us. How unnatural it can be to see in ourselves what God sees in us. What we think we are worthy of versus what He already has strategically and profoundly planned for us. But little did humble Mary know the crucial impact she would have regardless of how she saw herself. And little do we know what we are capable of doing and becoming because we are His.

We've got it all backward, you see.

We spend so much time pleading for things to be over or things to be different, whether situational or about ourselves. We see our differences as a weakness or a setback, but what so many fail to recognize is that it is exactly what is different about us that we need to grow in. It's our individual differences that make progress, success, and change for the better. If we were all the same, how stupid would that be? We as humankind literally wouldn't get anything done.

Now being a completely tattooed public speaker for the Church of Jesus Christ might seem ironic and impossible, but I'm doing it. I create. I write. I speak. I progress. I grow. I conquer. I win. I surprise. And I make things happen because I have never been told that I couldn't, not by myself and most definitely not by my God. Because it is exactly my differences, it is exactly my hurdles that I explained above, that have brought me to everything I have and am doing now. It is everything that makes me different that has made me help others and succeed in finding a purpose far bigger than I ever could have imagined. And I hate to imagine it any different.

I'm tired of having other people tell me how my life should be. I don't have time to let other people's experiences and advice dictate my decisions. I'm only living this mortality thing once, and I'm not letting someone else pick for me.

Getting engaged and becoming pregnant, among other things, were just overwhelming in an eye-opening way. Don't let people tell you marriage becomes boring. Don't let people tell you kids ruin or take away from things. Don't let people's comments of, "Once you get married, you can't . . ." and "Once you have kids, you won't be able åto . . ." I absolutely love everything about having kids. Adventures have doubled since we had them because we chose to plan it that way. And I, more than anything, love being married. I do. I love it. I don't think people say it enough. I think life is hard, but marriage makes those hard things in life easier. Marriage freakin' rocks! Because we consciously choose, every day, to make it that way and to work toward that. Life is better experienced with someone else. Experiences are richer when shared. Trials are easier as a team. Strength is there when you are weak. Humor is perfectly there for the good and the bad. A change of course is more of an adventure. Learning new things from them, and with them, is magic. And the growth you experience over the years is the gem in life.

The point is, don't let others tell you that because you look a certain way, or did something differently, or any other factor, you cannot do or accomplish or succeed. Because they simply are not true. If I were to listen to comments and advice like that, perhaps I wouldn't be here writing this or any other book. Perhaps I would have listened and conformed to the labels of "irony" and "impossible," and who knows whose life I would have actually been living, because it wouldn't have been mine or the one God intended for me.

Christ did not die on a cross just for us to sit around and let others dictate living a fuller life! He didn't die on a cross for us to pick ourselves apart or compare ourselves to others or not do that one thing because so-and-so didn't do it or for any other reason we hear from others. We don't have time for that. We have work to do! And I promise you that work can be done from where you are with whatever you have, exactly how you are.

Life is what we choose to make of it. Life is what we make time for. And we should make time for whatever we want to and not be influenced by what others say and how they choose to spend their time. Choose adventure! Choose passion. Choose to act on those recurring crazy thoughts. Choose to find and make the time, because we have time for whatever we choose to make a priority. We should, every day, choose the things we love and choose the things we feel called to do.

We really can make things happen exactly as we are and *where* we are. Because it is passion that overrides any lack of skill we may think we have, or shortcomings we focus on, or whatever. Because it is God who overrides the "impossible." Because it's through those recurring thoughts, even if they may seem ironic or crazy, that our souls are trying to guide us to the life we were meant to live all along.

And I get it. I totally, 100 percent, get it. It's easy to feel on the verge of losing our minds because we think, *Oh my gosh, if one more person posts that they are going to Disneyland for the ump-teenth time—or What on earth, seriously? How are they going out of the country again? Must be nice, huh.*

Seems like everyone else is always out exploring or renovating or up-sizing or accomplishing, and you just look at yourself . . . sitting in your home . . . with things going very differently than what you're seeing from everyone else . . . leaving us feeling disappointed at things that actually shouldn't be disappointing at all.

Discontentment makes dangerous and easy grounds for the adversary to run rogue with our thoughts, our lives, and our purpose. Overlooking the blessings of our "ordinary" lives. Unconsciously rejecting the daily things God brings to us to show He is there, He is mindful, and He is uniquely crafting them very specifically and personally for us.

I don't know, maybe everyone else isn't the problem. Maybe it's not them, even if we feel justified. The more I seek for enlightenment on this for myself, the more I realize it has nothing to do with anyone else and it has everything to do with me. Here's what I've learned:

We really are in control of how we act and react. We really do find what we look for—the good or the bad. And you know, for my first little bit in my new state unrealistically wearing my fake skin sleeves, I think it would be safe to say I was looking for the bad more than the good, even if that was unconscious.

That girl whose life you want, you probably don't *really* want her life. You don't know the depths of her past, present, or future. You don't know her soul's splinters and heartaches. You don't know her struggles, trials, pleadings to God, or her full story. Before we compare ourselves to someone else, remember that another person out there is probably comparing themselves to us. But most important, remember who created you. The most perfect being to ever exist. A perfect god who does not make mistakes. Remembering that it's those differences that separate us, and the things that separate us from being all alike are essential to getting things done! It's how we soar. It's what God perfectly crafted, unique to each of us, for divine reasons of growth and success.

And maybe it's not always about discontentment. Sometimes those thoughtful and reflective moments about what we're doing and what we have can be productive and not destructive, depending on if the Spirit is there. Self-reflection is incredibly vital for the Spirit to redirect and teach and counsel and confirm and tell you what your focus should be, not distracted and confused by others.

It's incredibly important to do that self-check-in regularly with God to make sure we're on our best paths, or else I think we're missing the point and missing the undiscovered better blessings.

And I get it, we have these moments when we feel like everyone is crushin' life and we're just like, "*Well, cool, I don't know what I'm doing over here, lolololol.*" And we start to wonder if we're doing the right things or as many things, or if we're failing or falling or that our calling in life isn't grand enough or our impact isn't deep enough. And then we get in this weird dance with the adversary that can easily turn a downward spiral into a ditch of despair.

"Pick apart your body, judge others, and try to earn my love" are words Jesus never said. And yet sometimes we do this thinnnnggg, and we get it all weird and backward and it's confusing and complicated and we wonder and doubt and falter, and all thanks to the adversary, reality is often skewed and truths are often bent, and then we see that looking beyond the mark is dangerously subtle.

Isn't it wild to know that the adversary gets into our heads sometimes more than our actions? But the next time the adversary has another pathetic attempt to slow us down and bring us down, remember to recognize it's him and then not justify his presence. We shouldn't justify him being in our heads. We don't have to surrender and allow him to dictate our happiness or how we see and act. Force yourself to say a prayer, no matter how frustrated or down or confused you may be. Because regardless of whatever "crooked path" we unconsciously find ourselves sometimes on, we have a literal power to cast him out, a power he has to obey.

Because the straight truth and actual reality is that Christ is real, and He is ours. Because regardless of how real and subtle the adversary's pathetic attempts are, the reality is, they're still pathetic. Because regardless of his pathetic yet dangerously subtle attempts, that can't take away from the reality that light always overcomes dark, if we make the effort to turn on the switch. Comfort and truth are always there because Christ really does live and really is always there. With outstretched arms.

And how God sees us is the only thing that matters, and He sees us as someone capable of becoming like Him. And that is the ultimate reality and greatest pick-me-up. A universal fact, comparison is a poison we choose to drink. Perfect does not exist. And easy does not exist. But—optimism does. Hope and faith does. God does.

And you know what, the blessings in our "ordinary lives" are real blessings from a real god who really does love us and really did handpick those exact things to help us succeed gloriously and is preparing a place in heaven for you this exact moment. I'm not sure what part of that seems ordinary or insignificant or what part of it could make us feel anything but empowered. Because if that isn't empowering, then I don't know what is. Let's not allow anything or anyone to alter the fact that we are God's and we are made for something so much greater than just what's here.

And yeah, people are mean, and that stinks. Especially when they belong to the same church as you, because you feel like they should know better and because we should all be in this together.

There's nothing I hate more than when my integrity and intentions are assumed and exploited by strangers. There's nothing worse than when your entire character is destroyed by people you'll never meet and when inaccurate information about you in unfamiliar groups spreads around as truth and you have nothing you can do to defend or explain yourself. And even if you did, it would only make things worse. Because the thing about contention is, contention doesn't listen. No matter how perfectly crafted your response is, it's never interested in learning; anything said is just giving it another opportunity to get another jab in.

There is nothing worse than when despite your prayers and personal revelations and efforts to clarify, to help, to be transparent, to inspire and triple check it all, many seem to always miss the point and get it wrong and tear you down.

There will always be someone waiting to get offended by something because they hold the world to their own personal expectations. Sometimes we just need to step back and worry about ourselves and worry about God and go onward and upward in the best way we know how.

Because although it is exhausting and although it is heavy—and wow, is it oh so tempting to slow down or to quit—we only get to do this mortality thing once, and life is too short to get worked up and worried about things we have no control over. Because what happens when we slow down or stop or dismiss or second-guess? The adversary wins.

And let me clarify something so important that I have learned in my many states of residency and my practically every single state and five countries of travel and my very in-depth study of religious cultures outside of my own: Judgment is not a Latter-day Saint thing. High expectations are not a Latter-day Saint thing. Broken standards are not a Latter-day Saint thing. It is not exclusive to my, or any, religion. And if I have learned anything from living on the east coast as a non-member for twenty-one years and traveling non-stop for nine years and counting, it's exactly that. Hate, hurt, judgments, standards, offense, and expectations are most definitely not a Latter-day Saint thing; they're a human thing. They live *everywhere.*

If we think parents getting disappointed for their child not living up to their expectations doesn't happen anywhere else; if we think experiencing body shaming by dressing differently doesn't happen in any other religion; if we think broken expectations within families, or the workplace, or from mentors, doesn't happen anywhere else; if we think broken hearts and broken families from choosing a different path doesn't happen anywhere else; if we think people saying they will do one thing then living another doesn't happen anywhere else—then perhaps we have bigger problems.

I do know how hurtful it can be. We expect more from members of our congregation because we "know" they have been taught differently. I know it can hurt more when we are supposed to be in this together. But what if our offense is improperly directed? Our stumbling block is that we assume. We assume others feel what we feel, and we assume our opinion is always correct and justified. And we assume everyone has been taught what we have been taught and that everyone knows what we know. But if we don't think this is hurtful to anyone else, especially when coming from family or the community—then perhaps we have bigger problems.

The reality is that it's hurtful no matter who we are, where we are, or what religion we may belong to. Because that, too, is a human thing. And the reality is, no matter age, race, gender, religion, sexual orientation, or location, we really are all in this together! The profound fact that we really are brothers and sisters has no bounds. So, before we take our hurt feelings from others and turn them into pointed fingers and inaccurate conclusions, before we take false accusations from others and let them stop us from doing what we should, before we improperly direct our offense, before we take our broken hearts and loneliness and blame God and blame His Church—let's take a step back.

Let's remember that no "worldly" experience can take away from the incredible power of love. That no action from man can take away from the incredible power and reality of God. That no hurtful comment or untrue jab from someone else can take away from the reality and importance of His command for us to forgive all and keep going. No broken standard or sin or different path can take away from the unchanging truth that we are *all* His.

Has someone done or said something really hurtful to you? Same. And as much as I wish I could swing a wand so everyone can see others how God sees us and understand the Atonement a little better, I can't. But as I found myself eye-rolling again just the other day because of how cruel people can be, the best advice I can give you is to just worry about yourself and worry about God. We absolutely should not let it ever stop us from living the eternal truths that affect our forever. We can't change others, but we can change ourselves. We can change how we react to others and how we let it affect us and how we live here and hereafter.

And yeah, maybe people are mean to me still, but you know what is different now from years ago? *Me.* I'm different. Not them. And when I hear or read or notice those things, I don't respond. I shrug it off and move on. And so should you. Those comments or looks from others should have no effect on us because in reality, they absolutely do not matter, because of the reality of Christ and who He sees us becoming and what He is capable of helping us move past.

So, when yet another time someone says something mean to us, intentionally or not, here's what we need to do: we keep trying. We keep going. We keep going to church. We keep reading the scriptures. We keep praying. We keep going to the temple. We keep turning to God. We keep smiling. Keep laughing. Keep doing you. And keep loving, serving, trusting, and turning to God.

Because nothing is worth giving up our forever happiness.

When we listen to negativity, we're giving permission to and allowing the adversary in, and he purposely ruins everything. Holding on to those things is only hurting us and our souls! Whatever it is that someone else hasn't learned yet cannot take away from the truthfulness of this church. Because no untrue or ignorant jab from someone else can take away the fact that this is all real. Our trials, our circumstances, our likes or followers, how other people are living, what other people are saying, how other people see us, or what season we're currently in will never alter the unchanging truth that the gospel really is true. God really is real. You really are His child. Christ really did die for you. The Atonement really did happen and covers everything. And your forever depends on how you live right now.

You get to decide how your day should be. Decide to be happy today, even in your trials and with other people's shortcomings. Decide to stay focused on what really matters and what affects your eternity. Decide to love and be an example, rather than judge and scold. Love yourself and take care of your soul! Decide to laugh a lot and follow God. Take time every day to tell Him everything. Invest in the time to ask questions and dig a little deeper and look a little longer. Don't let a bad day make you feel like you have a bad life.

Let go of any hurt or weight caused by someone who is oh so human. Because contention never listens, and we don't have time for Satan's pathetic games. Because other people's perceptions of us ain't none of our business, if we are right with our souls and with the Lord.

Absolutely nothing is worth turning away from the most powerful being to ever exist. Because we are all oh so human, and we really are all in this together. Because it's living the gospel that matters. It's thriving in who you really are and who God wants you to become that matters. It's making sure we aren't letting anything affect our forever that matters. It's feeding and taking care of the eternal soul living within us that matters.

Let's do everything we can to continue to grow and strengthen our testimonies so that nothing will shake them. Let's always keep our focus on Him so that nothing will take us away from living the beautiful principles of the gospel. Let's just worry about ourselves and worry about God so that we will never deprive ourselves from living the way He wants us to—the only way to experience real and lasting happiness.

Because it's not, and never will be, about comparing yourself to anyone. It's about your life being okay, too. However it may be. In case no one else is telling you, whatever you're doing is great. And it is right for you and your family and the season you are in. Whatever your situations and circumstances are, it is enough. You are not any less of anything because of them. In case no one else is telling you, you and your efforts are important. They matter. They don't go unnoticed. And God knows and understands and blesses you in the capacity you're in.

I want to be the one to tell you, in case no one else does, that your life has purpose. It has deep meaning. It has godly help and support available at every stage of your life. And we do not need to be any more of anything to feel of Him, to be loved by Him, and to receive the best ever created by Him. Let's always celebrate you not being "typical." Celebrate and embrace and be proud of your differences. Being different is an amazing gift!

Celebrate with confidence knowing that the best thing we could ever be is ourselves and who God wants us to be. Celebrate knowing He is in charge and He does not make mistakes. Embrace yourself, your life, and your role—whatever it is that it may be. Embrace and love who you are and where you are. There is something amazing and needful and profound at every stage of our life.

Keep being you. Keep laughing. Keep praying. Keep trying. Don't exhaust yourselves to live up to this "perfect" image *someone* else created for your life. Stop thinking perfect is a thing, and don't drink the poison of comparison. Because life is too short not to love the journey God has for you. Because life is too short to not give chance to the crazy and allow God the opportunity to show us how great He really is. Because life is too short not to see yourself the way He sees you. And who He sees you as is someone capable of becoming like Him.

Because life is too short to feel lousy for an unworthy reason. Too short to play "keep up." Too short to get worked up over things that don't matter. Too short to be influenced negatively over people you'll never meet. Life is too short to allow the adversary to drive our lives or our self-worth and purpose into the ditch. Too short to forget that we have the most powerful being to ever exist, on our side, who never leaves if we but look for Him above our desires and above the bad and the distracting.

Because life is just too short to be anything but happy.

I hope you feel empowered by exactly who you are. Because with God, you have all the power. Absolutely never forget who you are and whose you are. Absolutely never forget that you have divinity inside of you. Your God, a perfect Creator who crafted worlds without number, felt the need to create and perfectly craft you. Needed. Wanted. Essential. Our perfect Creator created you perfectly. That is the reality. That is power.

You have a god. You have a god who is yours, who never leaves you. A god who has all the power in existence on your side to help you succeed and become better and to conquer the world. How cool is it that the same being who created galaxies without number looked at you and decided the world needed you too? And if having an all-knowing, all-powerful god on your side giving you the ability to overcome the world is not empowering, then I don't know what is.

Let's vow to do a better job and quit knocking ourselves down. Because regardless of how we see ourselves, God sees us for who we truly are, like Mary: Capable. Worthy. Crucial. And profoundly part of something so much better than we could ever imagine! We are His and that is everything. Whatever you're doing in the season you're currently in, remember: YOU DESERVE TO BE HAPPY. YOU DESERVE TO BE LOVED. YOU DESERVE TO BE VALUED. YOU DESERVE TO SUCCEED AND DO THE IMPOSSIBLE. And in case no one else is telling you, THE WORLD WILL NOT BE BETTER OFF WITHOUT YOU! Let us live the life we're destined to live, one hand-picked by God.

We find what we look for. Look for the good. Look for God.

CHAPTER 10

When We Keep Looking Back

I WAS HEADED OUT for another speaking engagement, but living in upstate New York during the time, and accessibility to fly anywhere was tricky. Direct flights from my local airport just didn't exist for me. It'd take, most times, three planes and a day just to get me there and then repeat it all on the way back. I was on my way to Vegas and had already been traveling for the entire day because with accessibility and layovers, that's what was available. As you can imagine, the plane going to Vegas was *huge*. Those plane rides are always different than other plane rides; they're loud and filled with excited friends traveling in big groups who usually start to party while on the plane, or even right before. I was in the back of this giant plane and it had taken two hours for the snack cart to come down by where I was sitting. There was a woman diagonal to me wearing headphones, who was getting not only impatient but mad because of the long wait. And I mean *mad*. This was the start of her vacation, and the two-hour wait had ruined her vision of her plane ride to order drinks during the flight and kick it off the way she wanted. A cart was finally coming, but it passed right by. I assumed the cart needed to be restocked, but I saw a cart behind that one that looked just fine, making the usual rounds row by row. But this woman, she didn't see the other cart behind the one that passed by, so she turned around to follow the first cart that had passed her, and she was hanging out in the aisle backward, mean-mugging the flight attendant. She stayed there with just the biggest disgruntled look on her face, hoping that the attendant would turn around and see the injustice that had happened. She had gotten so upset with this cart that passed her by, which was now in the alleyway, that she started swearing to herself, but purposely loud enough for others to hear. She had become so caught up over this, all while facing backward and hanging out in the aisle, that she didn't even see that other cart was now right behind her. She became so distracted that she didn't even realize that it was her turn to order with the other cart, but the attendant couldn't get by because she had her headphones on and was blocking the way, which ended up prolonging her wait for service because of it all.

I wonder how many times I've done this. I wonder how many times I've become distracted with how I wanted things to go that I completely missed everything else that's happening. I wonder how much time I've spent looking backward that I missed or prolonged what was coming. I wonder how many times I've unconsciously trapped myself because I'm stuck on this vision I made for myself that it becomes the reason why no progress has been made.

A new life as a convert is quite literally a new life. And I had to navigate this new life by myself. My family was upset and not talking to me, I lost every single one of my friends instantly because they wanted nothing to do with what I was a part of, and I worked the evening shift full-time, so those members that did live nearby were coming home from work and school just as I was leaving to start. It all happened so fast. I went from thinking I had my life all figured out to being forced to get comfortable with discomfort and all this alone time I now found myself having. I would get home from work every night at around 1:00 a.m., and I would drive to my studio apartment through the peak of the nightlife. I was surrounded by so many bars and clubs that the streets were just filled with people walking in the roads hopping around to all the different places. I would drive by a flood of groups of friends with their arms hooked to each other's and laughing so loud. I would make it to my apartment and hear the noise of laughter and music across the street from several porch parties, listening every Friday and Saturday night, every weekend. Now, it's not that I missed the nightlife—I didn't at all. That was never my scene anyway. But it was a clear and consistent reminder that everyone had friends to see and stories to hear and experiences to live. And there I was, alone. And I did not. And I would look back at how even just a few weeks ago things were not like that. I would look back in longing when I would walk to my dad's house every day and we'd do the crossword puzzle on his porch before I had to go to work. I would look back on having people call me asking what I was doing. I would look back on when things made sense and when things were comfortable.

When I was pregnant with my first, Gracie, I was very sick. I had to cancel all my speaking engagements for the entire pregnancy and would make multiple visits to the hospital throughout. And because of it all, I gained a lot of weight. I'm talking about a hundred pounds; I'm talking about an entire junior high student that I just accumulated. I'd never even had a headache before, but then I started to get these migraines that would make it difficult to function. I couldn't do anything that I was doing before. I wasn't able to do anything that made me me. I couldn't write in my journals and I couldn't blog because of my head. I couldn't speak and do firesides because of my health. And then I would look in the mirror, and I didn't even recognize myself. I didn't feel like me, and I didn't even look like me. This—was brutal. And the worst part was that I couldn't do anything about it. I felt it was out of my hands. Not only did I not like me, but I felt so guilty thinking about what kind of wife I was, thinking, *This is not who Ben married.* Of course, he never ever thought like that, but I did. As things came up that I couldn't do or that were hard for me, I would then start thinking of how things used to be and what we used to do. And it's not that I placed blame on me or anything else, but it's just that I missed it all so much. I missed speaking. I missed running. And writing. And staying awake past 8:30 hanging out with my husband. And being able to make it through a sacrament meeting. I missed me and how everything was before this pregnancy made me so sick. I just wished life could have been how it used to be. I hated the season I was in.

I can think of a bunch of times when I've had these thoughts. Most of my trials, I think. When things are hard, when things are unwanted, when things are unplanned, we wonder, and we reflect on when things weren't like that. Sometimes it's productive and sometimes it's destructive; and when it's done in the wrong spirit, the adversary is quick to step in and take our thoughts and our efforts and purpose in a steep downward spiral. And like the woman on the plane upset about the missed snack cart, or in better terms, our missed visions and desires, the adversary can run rogue with our thoughts and perspectives to distract or blind us from the blessings and the opportunities that are there or that are quickly coming.

During one of my unwanted and undesired situations, I was pleading to God so much that I completely exhausted myself. Ever have times when you're so tired that everything then seems hard and stinky and it's like a downward spiral of a mess? Most days within the hard and unwanted I find blessings and things to laugh at within my personal trial, but then some days—like this particular time—I crumble. I cry. I break down. I become overwhelmed with burden and am dragging with those thoughts of all the things I wish were different. I cried on my stairs out of exhaustion and frustration. And then I put a pillow over my face as I complained to Ben about my struggles. I woke up the following day with mascara on my forehead and my arms and my neck. But no matter how dim things seemed in that moment, God spoke peace to me. But it wasn't during the time I was yelling at Him wondering where He was. And it wasn't during the time I was pleading for things to be over or things to be different. It was the time when I was lying on the floor in prayer, exhausted, in silence. The Spirit always speaks, but it's up to us to listen—and not just listen for what we *want* to hear.

God reminded me of the talk by Elder Holland where he, too, was going through one of those times when we wish that things were different. He and his just recently married wife, Patricia, were both students at BYU. They were going through some financial problems, and their situation seemed to be heavy and their options and future seemed dim. Elder Holland said, "Honey, should we give up? I can get a good job and carve out a good living for us. I can do some things. I'll be okay without a degree. Should we stop trying to tackle what right now seems so difficult to face?" He told his wife, "Let's go back. Let's stop all this and go home because the future holds nothing for us."

Remembering Lot's wife, Elder Holland said, "She doubted the Lord's ability to give her something better than she already had. Apparently she thought—fatally, as it turned out—that nothing that lay ahead could possibly be as good as those moments she was leaving behind."

Then, as I was sitting on the floor covered in mascara, my soul was pierced with energy as I thought of Sister Holland's reaction. She grabbed him by the collars—at a time where they, too, were questioning their situation and their future and considering giving up—as she looked him square in the eye and spoke boldly. "The future holds *everything* for us."[58]

My heart started to race and I felt this jolt of energy run through my body, but it wasn't energy; it was my soul coming *alive* for the first time in months, it seemed. It was almost as if God Himself was grabbing *me* by the collars, looking *me* in the eyes, and telling *me* boldly that, truly, the future holds *everything* for us.

So you know what? Yeah, maybe things really stink for you right now. Yeah, maybe you wish things were going differently. But you know what? The future holds everything for you. "Faith builds on the past but never longs to stay there. Faith trusts that God has great things in store for each of us."[59] And you know what? We don't have to wait for the trial to end or for a new day to come, and relief doesn't have to be postponed until a trial is over; it can come with a change of mindset. A mindset of hope. A mindset that allows us to see past our narrow views and mortal desires. Relief can come with the realization that you're still here and you are not broken.

---

58. Holland, "'Remember Lot's Wife.'"
59. Holland, "'Remember Lot's Wife.'"

It can come from seeking and noticing the small but significant blessings from God that show He is there. Relief is always there because God is always there.

I get it. I get those times when we are craving a fast-forward button, or even a rewind button. And it doesn't necessarily have to come from long trials, but just from bad days or unfulfilled desires.

You know those bad days where one thing after another, it seemed, goes wrong or gets worse? And it's not even anything specific that is going wrong—sometimes it's just a day built of lots of little things that add up too quickly too soon. During one of those particularly bad days that I couldn't quite put my thumb on why exactly it was bad, just a lot of those little things, before lunch had even come, I, myself, stopped trying do a single thing to try and make it better. I just let it happen and even expected more things to go wrong. I watched the clock, *slowly* counting down until the day ended. I just wanted the day to end and be over and start again tomorrow.

At 8:30 p.m., I was sitting at the kitchen table typing some thoughts. I find I'm most productive with my thoughts through writing. Ben came into the room and grabbed my arm to try and pull me up. I fought against his attempt to make me do anything other than what I was attempting to do. He pulled again, signaling for me to stand up, but I was right in the middle of doing the only thing I wanted to do in that moment: escape from the chaos of the day and write a few things down. I felt like I had no control over my day, and Ben was now trying to take me away from the one thing I had control over doing, writing.

He pulled one more time, and I knew if I didn't get up at this attempt, he'd sigh, leave me alone, and go into the other room. He'd leave me alone and let me do whatever it was that I was doing. But, see, I love Ben. I love him enough that I didn't want to make him feel bad for trying to help and reach out. I surrendered and I stood up. He then started slow dancing with me in the middle of our kitchen. Do you believe that? Dancing in our kitchen.

No, it's not like out of the movies, it wasn't cute to me. I thought it was *so* silly at first to slow dance with no music. It was awkward, and I was not in the mood. But here he was as the night was settling down, attempting to change my day. It was 8:30 p.m., and he was trying to change my *day*—can you even do that? Is that even allowed?

It worked. *Oh*, did it work. It wasn't long before everything that was bothering me and slowing me down and deflating me and my energy and spirit *disappeared*. Even that late at night, we pressed the restart button. And I think there's something to that. I think we forget we *can* do that, we *can* change things and we *should*.

We have a God of endless chances and a God who is always there to help. Every passing minute is a chance to turn it all around, if we lay aside our pride and *stand the heck up*. Take the hand of the things trying to pull us away from our slumps.

One of the years I was speaking on tour at Time Out for Girls, I tried to teach this, but part of me really learned it visually during these events. After a two-day conference for teen girls, I was the concluding speaker. I spent two whole days watching a few thousand girls cry, laugh, open up, pray, sing, change, and recommit. I told that story of Ben and I dancing, and then I made them all stand up and *dance*. I got off the stage and I went into the crowd with them and I shook it in ways I don't normally shake it. I got them to dance and try moves they've never done before, and *man* did it get them laughing. Everyone was moving, even the shy girls and the girls who came by themselves. And in that moment, even if it was just for a moment, we were all able to step away from, and forget, whatever it was that was keeping us down. In that moment, no matter what we were struggling with, we were able to laugh and *let go*.

When the song ended and I made it back on stage, I had every single girl hook arms with the girls next to her. We took a really big inhale and let out a slow exhale. I told them to look around. To see what I could see. Thousands of girls linked together. To point out the reality that we are part of something so much greater than what's just here. We are part of something so much greater than the here and the now and our current situation. Because of Christ, there is always someone or something there to grab us and pull us higher. Because of Him, there is always something to dance about. Comfort, guidance, renewal, strength, a chance to change, and a chance to start again are always there because Christ really is always there. And it is never too late to allow things to change and take a new direction and a new course.

Are we trapping ourselves? Are we selling ourselves short? Have we surrendered to our circumstances? Have we fallen victim to things going different than we envisioned for ourselves? Are we allowing the adversary to unnecessarily linger longer and keep us standing still? Are we spending too much time pleading for things to be over or things to be different that we are distracted from and missing the here and the now? Like the woman on the plane, are we spending too much time looking back that we are missing what is in front of us? Are we acting on the reality of the things asked of us to do daily? Are we taking hold of those the resources and people and help that are trying to bring us to greater heights? Is there something that we can let go of?

There will always be something hard to overcome or something new to figure out. How unproductive it is to crave a rewind button or to long to live in the future. How dangerous it is to hold on to this make-believe mortal vision we created in our minds. It is unhealthy for us and our souls, and before we know it, life will have passed us by, empty. And we allowed it to happen. And we will have missed so much, and it will be too late.

Enjoy today. Today, right now, is the best place to be. Happiness, opportunities, and blessings *do* await us in *this* day. Right now. Because every day at every stage of our lives we have God. Search, learn, and find joy in your trials and in your bad days, because surely there will be many. Be productive with your time and that which you do have. Look for the good—it is always there. Good is always there because Christ is always there. Because "until you give up on the idea that happiness is somewhere else, it will never be where you are."[60] What if trials are actually the gems in life, creating and bringing us to the absolute best and most fulfilling journey? What if our loneliest days are perhaps when God is closest to us? What if our hardest days are, in fact, rich with direction, lessons, and guidance that move us forward, not backward, on the path God has set for us? Let's turn our trying times into productive learning times.

Let's not forget perhaps one of the most important blessings He has given us: joy! God wants and intends for us to be happy. Let's take joy in our hard times. And take joy in being taught, in growth, in progression, in change, and in the strengthening process. Maybe you're in a hard or unwanted or a different-than-everybody-else phase right now, but we have Godly help and support available at every stage of our life. And we do not need to be any more of anything to feel of Him, to be loved by Him, and to receive His help. Embrace yourself, your life, and your role, whatever it is that it may be. There is something amazing and needful and profound at *every* stage of our life. Keep laughing. Keep praying. Keep trying. "Tell them to fear not, for God will deliver them."[61]

So what do you need to let go of today? Yes, even if it's late into the night. It's allowed. You can start over, and you absolutely do not have to just accept that today is *just a bad day* and hope for a better one tomorrow. Today, right now, there is something to dance about. Motivation and comfort and guidance and energy and a new mindset are a prayer away. All is *not* lost. Because today, right now, God is there, and He is *yours*. On hand and ready to pull us up.

All we need to do is reach because, truly, the future holds everything for you.

60. Hank Smith, *Be Happy* (American Fork, UT: Covenant Communications, 2017), 12.
61. Alma 61:21.

CHAPTER 11

When We Need to Change

FROM WHAT I WAS PICKING UP when learning of the Church, God expects certain things from us, and He expected something different and something better from me and how I was currently living. And that meant a lot of change needed to happen. Really hard, completely torn-down and rebuilt, kind of change. I didn't grow up in the Church, I didn't have family I could turn to for counsel and their experiences, and those I saw on Sundays either lived too far away or conflicted with my evening work shifts. It was me, and that was it. I was left to myself and Church pamphlets and *a lot* of experimenting on how everything worked and *a lot* of conscious *daily* effort to know if it was right.

I didn't know how to pray, I barely had even heard other people pray, but I just did it because I knew I should. I am certain my first prayers were quite literally the worst prayers Heavenly Father has ever heard. And who knows what I was reading about from the scriptures. They made no sense to me for a while because the language was so foreign, but I read them because I knew I should. And even though my motives were skewed, I acted and put in effort, even if my effort was what I was *sure* was the worst God had ever seen.

The Sacred Grove was where I said my very first prayer ever. I would have lessons with the elders in the Sacred Grove, which may seem really cool, but when you don't know what the Sacred Grove is, it's more like, "Why did we drive to the woods in the middle of no-where?"

I always thought religion was only something people turned to when things were going wrong in their lives as some sort of emotional comfort . . . right? And here I was thinking I could conquer the world myself. No matter how silly and uncomfortable and foreign it was to me, I prayed and read the Book of Mormon daily. No matter how awkward it was and no matter how much I felt like I didn't fit in at first, I went to church every week. You know, to prove them wrong. And I made sure I was going to do those things long enough to allow room for contrast and change to happen. It couldn't be a one-and-done deal.

Despite my motives, despite how I felt about religion, despite feeling content with how my life was, despite feeling confident and happy with the direction I envisioned for myself, I was wrong. I changed. Not because someone told me I had to and not because I was unhappy. I changed because that is what happens when we actually live the simple teachings of the gospel. I changed because that's what happens when we try. No matter how awful and awkward and skewed our efforts may seem to us, we are absolutely blessed by every effort of trying. Every single step we take closer to Him is noticed and magnified and blessed. I changed because that's what happens when Christ becomes a reality to us; we change because then we want to, and because then *we can.*

The most intimate thing we could ask someone to do is get baptized. Because when we ask that, we're asking them to change almost everything—not just what they do, but even the way they think. It's an invitation to leave behind years of habits, many traditions, and some-times family and friends. It's overcoming and relearning and a deep, deep reconstruction of themselves.

It can be overwhelming to gain a testimony. Change is extremely scary when you have such a long history and contrast of life filled with decisions, plans, paths, and dreams completely out of sorts with the Lord's will. Thinking of everything you need to be doing better or stop doing altogether is exhausting in and of itself. You have racing thoughts of fear of what this could mean for your life now and how unexpected and unknown and scary the next steps are. Especially—like so, so many who stand at their baptism—alone. Where "ward family" is literal family to so many. All while still learning how all this stuff works.

My very first church I attended when investigating and got baptized in was actually in a tiny building that used to be a small post office. It was so little we didn't even have pews. When you would walk in for church, you would grab a fold-out chair with you from the doorway to sit on for sacrament meeting. But that little singles branch in that little old post office was the start of everything. I have never felt more welcomed anywhere in my entire life than in this building, where "*all are welcome*" really is practiced and you see it every single Sunday.

I am what happens when we don't judge someone. I am what happens when we try to live how Christ has taught us to. I am the result of unconditional love. A saved eternal soul, like mine, is a result of putting aside pride, assumptions, and fears. They sat next to me when I reeked of smoke. No one gave me any looks when I didn't know you were supposed to wear a dress, and they all hugged me anyway. When I didn't own a dress and defaulted to a black strapless sundress you wear over a bathing suit because it was all I had, they invited me to activities. They included me. They taught me.

Mostly, they unconditionally loved me regardless of my intentions, my appearance— anything. Even though I wasn't initially looking for a church to join, I was shocked because of how I was treated. Living in New York, I didn't think such nice people existed. It was, in every sense, the type of perfection that the people living the gospel should emulate. I am a devoted member, with all the covenants made and an eternal family started because in that building, no one judged me. No one forced me. In this building, we really were family. I was "alone" in the gospel in regard to my family and friends who left me, but I had them, and it really was everything to me. I have everything I have now—I am where I am now—because of that building. It is where I (and many others) started my forever with effects well into the eternities, with ripples far too great to comprehend. That building and the people in it are the gospel in action.

I have also been in wards where it was the complete opposite. I've been in wards where the stares felt like lasers coming in every direction. Wards where people really did say to me *how ironic it was that I was there with a Church book* because of how I looked. I really truly have received multiple emails over the years being told from members that God could never love someone like me. Coming from my first little church building to *that* was a faith crisis. How can you go to church when you don't feel comfortable there? How can you keep going when the people there hurt you? How hard it was at this time to have just been baptized, still with such a small sliver of knowledge of the gospel, and to experience that too frequently. If they only knew what *and who* I had to give up being there. All I had before was a ward family, but now I didn't even have that.

I struggled trying to figure out what I was going to do for a while. I had to make a decision. And it's a decision I had to make every day, sometimes several times a day, and that was, choose to get mad, choose to get hurt or bothered, or to choose . . . to not. To choose to keep going, choose to have faith and to trust, or to choose . . . to not. What it came down to, and what it always will come down to, is choose God. Choose God, or not. And I already chose who I wanted to follow, didn't I? That is what happens when you get baptized.

After months and months of pleading and praying, a different perspective came. I have given up much too much, and felt and experienced much too much, and have changed much too much to deny that God is reality. And that the covenants in the gospel are essential. And what is asked of us and how we act and react can affect our forever. And no mean comment or rude remark or lack of family, whether literal or spiritual, could change that reality. I know what life without the gospel is like—I went twenty-one years without it. There is nothing to offer to me. I am weak and not my best without it. The contrast is huge. The difference is real. Life without the gospel is not glamorous or cool. Was I going to let some person I didn't know stop me for doing what I knew was true? Is it worth giving up my eternal salvation? It wasn't. Nothing is worth giving up our eternal salvation. Nothing can take away the reality of God and His commandments and His promises and what life here and hereafter will be like if we choose Him, I don't care how many times a day.

I got an email from someone that started, "I was sitting in a lesson at church and the teacher said that all people with tattoos are bad people." She was hurt that that was being taught, but then she doubted how God saw her because, unknown to the woman who worked with her in Young Women, she too had tattoos. I receive way too many emails like this. *Why?* And no, this is not about tattoos but what should be a reality—that *everyone* is welcome to partake of the love and blessings of Christ. *Everyone* is welcome in this gospel!

It is never okay to teach hate. It is never okay to belittle and judge without even a glimmer of chance or fellowship shown. It's never okay to turn someone away. I'm tired of reading emails from people who want to get baptized but don't because they feel too different. Or don't because of how they were treated. I'm tired of reading literally thousands of emails from people saying they *want to come back* to church, but they're struggling to know how God sees them because of how they have been treated or because of mistakes they've made in the past.

But this is how we're sometimes teaching our youth to act and behave toward any that are different. What we say, what we are teaching, is literally shaping the future leaders and teachers and fellowship of the Church. And we are our own stumbling block. I don't care if you're covered in tattoos, I don't care what age or race or gender you are, I don't care if you grew up and stayed in the Church, or if you grew up and left the Church, or if you've never heard of the Church until now—*everyone* is welcome and invited to partake of forgiveness. Every single person is welcome and invited to partake of salvation. Of change. Of real happiness. Of the indescribable feeling of Christ's love.

Of His Atonement. Of a chance at a better life. And when we teach too much of the *what*, then it hinders too much of teaching what this is all about: the Atonement.

If only people knew how many messages I get every day from young teenage girls who struggle with pornography, maybe we wouldn't have teachers start out lessons with, "I know none of you do this, but..." And we can move past ignorance and hurt and unconscious judging and be more loving and productive with what the Atonement is all about. I have too many emails every day from people because they don't even know what that really means; they only know what they did was wrong.

I think we do a great job teaching how we should be living but not as great of a job teaching what we need to do when mistakes are made. So many are standing idle with terrible guilt not knowing what to do and needlessly feeling alone and like a bad person. *When do I need to talk to my bishop? What will that be like? How do I even repent? How do I use the Atonement? How can I change? How can I forgive myself?* This is what more lessons should be based around. Otherwise, we are our own stumbling block and little progress can be made. I know we'd like to think we know our peers and friends and our own children, but one of the most damaging things we can do is assume it could "never be my child" or "my young woman," because, unfortunately, it is. And unfortunately, they are all serving in callings and taking the sacrament out of immobilizing fear, shame, and lack of direction and counsel. We are hurting them by not teaching the resources the Lord has given us. We are hurting so many by assuming they know already, because too many of us of all ages and all lengths of membership don't. We are hurting them by not teaching the most important thing: Christ and His power and role in our lives. We are hurting ourselves by not taking advantage of it. How much better could things be if we not only teach but really understand and *know* personally too, the *why* and the *how*, and not too much the *what*. How many people would return and come back to church, or how many people could live a different life with lifted weight, if they knew what Christ really can do for us, if they knew the *why* behind all of this. The why behind the gospel and what's asked of us.

There's a video online of a comedian who, during his shows, likes to point someone random out of the audience and ask them who they are and what they do. He pointed to this one man and asked, and the stranger responded that he was a music teacher and he sings. The comedian puts him on the spot and tells him to sing "Amazing Grace," and he does and it's good. But then the comedian says, "I want you to sing it again, but give me the version of . . . you just got shot in the back..." So now this man re-sings "Amazing Grace," and *wow* does he sing it. It is the most beautiful, soulful version I have ever heard of it in my life. It was *so good* that the entire audience is cheering, and some are even crying, and some are standing out of their seats, and all are clapping! It really was so powerful the way he sang it, so much emotion in his face and power in his voice.[62] See, before, that audience member knew the *what*. But when he sang the second version, he knew the *why*. Great power comes from knowing our *why*.

Do we know our *why* in doing all of this? And if we don't know yet, are we doing something about it? Have we invested in the experiment to make it a reality to us and allow it to change us and take us somewhere better?

I hate the phrase "That's just who I am." When we think that, we deny the power of Christ and we hold ourselves back. Do not let who you used to be hold you back from who you can become. That is frustrating everything that the Atonement stands for and is. Christ's sacrifice and suffering would then be in vain. Be proud of the steps, no matter how small they seem to you, that you have taken to become better. Be proud that you are trying even if you aren't there yet. Every step, even the awkward or small or "worst He's ever seen" steps, that we take closer to Him, no matter how small or insignificant we may think it is, is noticed.

---

62. Michael Jr., "Know Your Why," Jan. 8, 2017, video, 3:49, youtube.com/watch?v=1ytFB8TrkTo.

To those of you with questions or doubts, are you actively doing something about them, or do you let them linger and hold you back? Are you remembering and doing the simple things of the gospel? To those who have been carrying too much weight for too long, for those who have things to move past, are you standing idle and letting the adversary win? Whatever you do, not doing anything is making things worse. No one can do it for you except you. It is through those simple things we have been taught first, whether in primary or by missionaries—prayer, scripture reading, church, sacrament, priesthood leaders, covenants, etc.—that we can know and stay strong throughout our lives. Why are we taught them first? Because the power that we are told that comes from doing those things is not wishful thinking. It's real.

And sometimes it's hard to see some of those blessings when we don't seem to "get anything out of it" every time we do those small things. I don't always remember what I learned from scripture study, and I don't remember what Sunday School was about last week. But I don't remember what I had to eat last week either, but I know I ate. Because if I didn't, I wouldn't be doing well. And without those small things daily that keep us and our souls going and healthy and strong, like eating, if we stopped doing them, we wouldn't be doing well.

With God, we have all the power. Absolutely never forget who you are and whose you are. Absolutely never forget that you have divinity inside of you. Your God, a perfect Creator who crafted worlds without number, felt the need to create and perfectly craft *you*. Needed. Wanted. Essential. Our perfect Creator created you perfectly. You have a God who has all the power in existence there to help you conquer the world! *Literally.* That is the reality. That is power. That is our *why.*

It's necessary to do some tearing down to rebuild. It's humbling and exhausting and discouraging, but I know if I'm not improving, I'm doing something wrong. As I was doing some soul stretching and making some changes just this week, I just felt so excited for repentance. Because it's not just for "sins" but for the little improvements to become a little better. Repentance isn't punishment and it isn't condemning.

Repentance is the *most optimistic* and hopeful thing to ever exist! It means all is not lost. It means we *can* change. It means we can improve. And oh man, would it stink so bad if we couldn't. It means hope and help and comfort are always there. It means *every passing second* is a chance to turn it all around. It means we are never alone. And really taking time and thinking about that and taking advantage of that fills me with actual goose bumps and humility and gratitude. "*I plead with you to correct your mistakes. Our savior died to provide you and me that blessed gift.*"[63]

And yet, like in the scriptures, people are living *as if no atonement had been made.*[64] Looking over the simple things asked of us, not knowing or understanding our *why*, allowing the adversary to come in many different disguises to get us to do what we know we should. Disguises that come in outfits of fear or hurt or anger or misunderstanding or laziness. He gets into our heads and into our hearts, telling us we aren't good enough, we aren't worthy to pray, we aren't worthy to come back. It is the adversary that tells that we are too far gone or all is lost. Or . . . well, the list of the adversary is a long list. *DO NOT HEED.*

Anything that is pulling us away and getting us to stand still is the adversary, and it's the adversary winning. Because if we think *God* will do anything to stop us from overcoming and conquering and returning to Him, we're wrong. Satan only has power to bruise. But bruises heal. With God we have the power to crush, and not just the adversary, but crush bad habits and past mistakes and so on. Please do not give up on the person you are becoming. Forgiveness and another chance are as oft as we need. And because of that love and fight He has for us, He says, "As often as my people repent will I forgive them."[65] Like the Lord in the vineyard, He is still here and ready for you to blossom.

"If you found out that the Savior was already on the earth, what would you desperately want to do today, and what would you be willing

---

63. Thomas S. Monson, "The Gift of Repentance," *Liahona*, Jan. 2018.
64. See Alma 11:41.
65. Mosiah 26:30.

and ready to do tomorrow?"[66] Let's take advantage of everything that has been given us because He *does* expect and want us back and has given us everything we need to do so. It may be a slow process, but giving up won't get you there any sooner. If you want a new tomorrow, then make new choices today. Don't wish for it; work for it. Have faith in the future and have faith in your God. Have faith, knowing that you are in the best hands. "Bring, save it be one soul unto me, how great shall be your joy with him in the kingdom of my Father!"[67] And how great will be your joy if that one person you bring is yourself.

A long time ago I received a priesthood blessing that said, "You are clean in front of Him. Heavenly Father does not see your tattoos. To Him, they are completely gone." That is the power and reality of Christ. That is why we are told to turn to Him. And it's not that God chooses to overlook our mistakes and sins and shortcomings; to Him, they *really are* gone. They don't exist. An actual clean slate. Can our mortal minds with memories even really comprehend that?

Let's not forget that *the importance of the Atonement is more powerful and more important than the* what, *or someone's past or outside appearance or mistakes or bad habits.* Let's not forget the beautiful reality that *Christ covers everything* if we turn to Him. We need to act and teach that no matter where anyone comes from, you belong here. Whatever you've been through, you are a part of this church. You belong. Whatever mistakes you've made or sins you've committed, you are not a bad person. You are loved. God's mercy will always be extended to you. A chance to change and be forgiven is extended to all.

Go back to the olive tree, but consider the *"poorest spot in all the land"* a little differently. Think of it as our past and who we used to be and what we used to do. If we remember correctly, those are the ones that brought forth the most fruit. No matter what circumstances we are coming from, even if we think it or whatever we have done is the worst there is, we can bring forth *"much fruit"* when we allow the

66. Wendy W. Nelson, "Becoming the Person You Were Born to Be," Gospel Media Library, Jan. 10, 2016, video, 10:39.
67. D&C 18:15.

Lord to help. We don't have to be who we used to be. We can grow into something different and really blossom. And that is one of the most important things.

The laborer in the vineyard asked if they should get rid of the branches that didn't seem to be doing well, but the Lord responds, "I will spare it a little longer, for it grieveth me that I should lose the trees of my vineyard."[68] So there they stay, and the Lord continues to stay there with it. Now is *not* the time for God to judge us, but to love and revive and forgive and correct and *change*. Now is the time for Him to fight for us and work with us and stay with us as much as He can and give us another chance. Because to the most powerful being to ever exist, we *matter*. And you are worth the effort and time and chances because He doesn't want to lose you. He is there knowing that good can always come with His help, even if it is coming from *the worst*—the worst sins, the worst backgrounds, etc.

Life without God is life without real happiness. But we won't know until we act. We can't know what it can do for us in our lives if we don't let it into our lives. We have to live it more fully to know more fully. He can't help us if we don't give Him anything to help us with. If it weren't for giving the gospel a real try, I wouldn't be here. I wouldn't have what I do. I would not truly be happy. I would not truly be me without it. Without Him. And it breaks my heart to imagine my life any different than what it is now.

Just because you may not believe in God does not mean He isn't always there and always loving you, ready to help and bless you if you just turn to Him. I hope that we will always allow ourselves to be changed by the gospel every day because, truly, it is *electrifying*! I continue to grow and be blessed by the gospel because of it. Because of Him and His ways. And as the world will continue to become even crazier as the last days approach, we can't afford to try it on our own and put our eternity and our souls in jeopardy.

Yeah, God asks us to do hard things. Sometimes He asks us to leave

---

68. Jacob 5:51.

our family and move across the country, like me. Sometimes He asks us to lose all our friends and be persecuted and judged, like me. Sometimes He asks us to do some soul stretching and completely torn-down and rebuilt kind of changes, like me. And sometimes it will take a lot of focus and fasting and crying, like me. But the best things can only come from following God. Hard times will consistently be there, but so will Christ, and with Him, we overcome and conquer absolutely everything! Every feeling of loneliness or doubt or confusion or addiction or bad habit. With Him we conquer the world!

To love it, we have to live it. We have to give this a real go! Every day. We have to continuously choose Him over the fleeting things of this world. We have to stay focused. Because we are meant for something so much greater than this, so much greater than the here and now, greater than the worldly "happiness" that isn't even a sliver of the godly and heavenly that's available to us.

How hollow life can be without experiencing it the way God intended. How painfully empty it will be to get to the judgment bar and realize life, and our chance at it, just slipped away from us and we can't do anything to get it back. Let's be driven by *why* we're really here and what we need to be doing. Let's recommit to act. Let's recommit to read. Let's recommit to study, really study. To learn. To turn to Him and talk to Him. To preach. To participate. To always exercise our change of heart muscle. And to keep going. Let's recommit to Him. To trusting Him, His commandments, and His path for us. Because every single bit of it is worth the sacrifice, the time, the trust, the loss. Because sacrifice, suffering, loss, etc. . . . , all of that doesn't even come close to what we receive in return.

To all of those wondering and wandering, answers and strength are there. Comfort, strength, energy, and hope are always there for us, because God and His resources are right there in front of us. And *wow,* what an indescribable difference I don't dare ever live without again. I don't dare give a pathetic attempt from the adversary one more second of my time because nothing is worth giving up what comes from what God has given us.

"Christ died from a heart broken by shouldering entirely alone the sins and sorrows of the whole human family.

"Inasmuch as we contributed to that fatal burden, such a moment demands our respect."[69]

And, might I add, demands our effort and time and dedication and love. He lived for us and He died for us so that we *can* change and become better. "His hand is stretched out, and who shall turn it back?"[70]

You are loved. You are not alone. You are not a bad person. The world will not be better off without you. All is not lost. "You have not traveled beyond the reach of divine love. It is not possible for you to sink lower than the infinite light of Christ's Atonement shines."[71] Help and healing and change and forgiveness are *always* there because Christ is *always* there. And He will never look at you like a waste of time.

God is not waiting to love and accept you until you reach some certain standard or qualifying factor. He will pick you up and put you on His shoulders because you, whoever you are, are absolutely worth it. You are worth everything God has to offer. He exists for you. To help you thrive and succeed and to become like Him. Please do not give up on the person you're becoming. No matter how long you have traveled in the wrong direction, you can always turn around.

Whoever's reading this: I hope you find happiness. Not temporary happiness, or the "if I pretend, maybe I'll be happy" kind, but long-lasting, real happiness that makes your face glow and lights up your soul. Happiness that comes from God, who is always there waiting for you and loving you and pleading your case. If you haven't yet, give Him the chance to show you how great your God truly is. Actively live the way we should to give Him the opportunity to show you the better way. And a better version of yourself, who you were meant to be all along.

---

69. Jeffrey R. Holland, "Behold the Lamb of God," *Ensign*, May 2019.
70. 2 Nephi 24:27.
71. Jeffrey R. Holland, "The Laborers in the Vineyard," *Ensign*, May 2012.

Let's make taking care of us and our souls a priority. Make God a priority. This gospel is not our last option—it is our *only* option. Because this isn't just wishful thinking. It's real. Real-life strength. Real-life promises. Real-life God. And once we know it, let's do everything we can to hold on to it and stay focused. Knowing that God is real and the gospel is true is another way of saying your life will never be the same, *but* it will be better. And yeah, we change. But when following God, we never change into someone else, but into our *real* selves—who we were meant to be all along. And the incredible thing about it all is starting a life of doing things you never thought you could do filled with better paths with better blessings with constant guidance. Because when we don't sacrifice living the gospel and we continue to put God first and trust Him, especially through change and confusion and sacrifice, we will never be shortchanged from the absolute best ever created. Because His promises are real. And He will show us. But we have to continuously put in the effort. "He is the light and the life of the world; yea, a light that is endless, that can never be darkened; yea, and also a life which is endless, that there can be no more death."[72]

---

72. Mosiah 16:9.

CHAPTER 12

When We Make It

BEN WAS AT OUR DINING ROOM TABLE when I got home from the gym, and he was just . . . sitting there. And it looked like he was maybe crying. I couldn't tell. I sat down and asked what was up, and he said, "*He did it again.*" Something happened, something one on one with Ben and God that brought him to just sit there soaking it all in with teary eyes.

Ben felt the previous week that he really needed to turn his scripture study into an active and intentional "*feast*" every day for that week, holding weight and surety that he knew something specific (but unknown) was going to come from it. And he really took that prompting with great dedication and wonder.

And because he did that, he and I actually received some pretty big counsel that week that left us sitting at our table together for two hours talking about everything he thought of and felt, as unexpected revelation and correction bringing us in a new direction just blossomed and unfolded to us both as we discussed together. It was then he told me about Nephi being asked to leave the promised land after years of sacrifice and wandering in the wilderness and establishing a new home in the land of Nephi. It was then that we started talking and planning on moving from New York. Are you losing count of how many times we've moved? Me too. After only being there a year, this never would have been something we sought after ourselves. It wasn't even an idea that would have ever crossed our minds on our own.

This move from New York back to Arizona ended up being two weeks without our moving truck and belongings. I was still pregnant with our third, and for two weeks we were sleeping on an air mattress on the floor and using the stairs as our table. I'm tired of moving and problem solving and starting over and sacrificing. I'm tired of never feeling settled because who knows what will come next.

But I quite enjoy doing the new and hard and unexpected right along with my family. What a thrill it is to see my kids learn independence and resilience and trust in the Lord, and to see what we all can be capable of doing at any age. I quite like seeing what we can overcome and seeing how we really thrive and how life can really blossom when we have faith in, and push through, what could seem like another unwanted burden to figure out or another trial to bear.

Confusion and conflict turned into a new and exciting path with determination and surety. Ben reads scriptures every day, but that week he was seeking *knowing* something new was coming. I wonder what I've missed in the past from not investing as much dedication and wondering, knowing something new was in fact coming, not just new insight to scripture stories, but personal revelation, new to my personal path. If we invest and if we are intentional, if we listen to subtle thoughts that come when we're seeking, if we pay attention to recurring ideas, if we take time to explore and talk spiritually with our family, if we invest in Heavenly Father, then we'll have these moments where we just... sit there. And with tears in our eyes we'll think, *He did it again.*

And then we'll move forward with determination and optimism through our unexpected correction and exciting change of courses as we let life blossom and allowing ourselves to let *God be God* in our lives.

My friend and author David Butler told a story in which he was teaching an investigator about the plan of salvation. And the man learning of the Church says something along the lines of, "Wait, you mean to tell me we lived with God before here?" *Yep.* "And we were happy?!" *Yep!* "So then, what? God just brought us here and dropped us off to see if we could make it back?"

Could you imagine if your dad packed you and your siblings up in the van and drove to the middle of the desert, kicked you out of the car, said, "Hope you make it home!" and then drove off? And that was it? Just some weird game to see if we can make it back?

Back in the days of Jesus, shepherds were considered dishonest, untrustworthy, unclean thieves,[73] which is totally ironic considering they had one of the most important jobs: raising and protecting the lambs that would be sacrificed for the temple, symbolically representing the Messiah, the ones that strictly needed to be clean and perfect in all ways, "*without blemish.*" Anything bad that happened to those sheep could cost the shepherds their lives. Leaving them could result in murder.

So yeah, it's cool the shepherds were believers and had an angel come and they were able to see the babe swaddled in a manger. But it's a little more impactful to me knowing they willfully abandoned the flock, left the most important job there was, knowing what it would cost them. Because to them, even the most important job wasn't as important as finding and following Christ. Because to them, it was more important to be closer to Him than it was to live. Because to them, they knew to truly *live* came from Him, the Light and the Life.

It dawns on me how I limit God and how I place restrictions on Him. What kind of life would we be living if, like the shepherds, we sacrificed a little more to come closer to Christ? What kind of counsel and exciting ride would we embark on if we invested a little more time to really seek Him and more moments that leave us saying, "He did it again"? What would change if our relationship with Him went from what we allow God to *be* instead of dictating what we want Him to *do*? What kind of life could we be living if we stopped keeping God at arm's length? What could our life look like if we trusted Him completely? What could we receive if we gave God the chance to show us how great He really is?

Unintentionally going for a Christmas theme, I think of the believers in 3 Nephi. There was a day set when all the believers were going to be

73. Eric D. Huntsman, "Why Shepherds Were Invited to Witness Christ's Birth—and Not Somebody Else," *LDS Living*, Dec. 19, 2016.

murdered unless the star came. They literally needed Christ in order to live. I can't imagine the fear most of them probably felt, or how many people may have started to doubt from all of the passing time between prophecies. Well, the sign *did* come, and in the perfect timing, too. It came the *very night* that was set for them to be killed. They were spared, and many converted. Like them, we too need Christ in order to really *live!*

The brother of Jared saw the Lord's finger, and that could have been great as is. But because of his strong faith and him actively seeking out and asking, he was able to see all of the Lord. Are we content with living life with finger miracles? Or by more fully trusting and proactively turning to God, are we going to allow ourselves to be shown *greater* things? By trusting more and proactively turning to Him, are we going to allow ourselves to be shown more of *Him*—all of Him, all that He has for us—and really *live?*

Because what if it's not just about getting by? What if it's not about just making it to the end? Because with God, there *are* more blessings, bigger miracles, and prosperity ahead. Are we going to go for it? Or are we going to "reject that Jesus, who stood with open arms to receive you!"?[74]

Brad Wilcox brought up the classic drawing people use for their church lessons with a hole in the ground and Christ as the ladder to get us. Brad explains just how inaccurate that drawing is. Christ doesn't just get us out of holes and bring us back to where we were; Christ is a ladder that brings us to *higher* places. Not to remain as we are, but to grow beyond where we were before. And so not only are we *not* just here to see if we make it back, but we are here to reach new heights that we would have never been able to reach otherwise!

Life has been wild since I joined the Church. I look back on all the trials I have been through, all the soul searching and soul stretching, deep loneliness, painful sacrifice and loss, feeling like it wasn't until baptism that I understood real pain. It wasn't until joining the Church that I felt I knew what indescribable anguish really meant because I've

---

74 Mormon 6:17

never struggled so long and so hard to a point that my body would literally ache. Times when I felt like I was being punished, times I felt overlooked, unimportant, forgotten. My point is, you're not alone. My point is, I know.

It's hard, I know. We have those times where we're losing our voices, losing hope, losing strength, not knowing if we even have the faith to keep going or not. But the optimism people may see from me, it's real. It's real strength, and real hope, and real happiness, and real smiles, because life *didn't* go the easy way, even though I wondered every second why I didn't. It's real because God has become real to me from it all.

Yeah, I know things can be really hard. Yeah, I know it could be easier to turn back. But I also know *how possible* it is and how worth it it is to keep going. The happiness you may see is not because my life is easy. Not because I don't still lose my voice yelling at Him still. It is literally the complete opposite. But because I know Him. Because of it all, I know God. And I love Him with a real love. And I couldn't trade that knowledge and relationship for anything.

I am by nature an optimist. But that doesn't mean you're happy all the time or that bad days don't come. It means that even on hard days, you know that it won't last, and better ones are coming, and there is something to learn and cherish during everything. It means you're proactive in your moments of crumbling and look for lessons and opportunities and light.

Having an abundant life is not a reflection of how many challenges we have, but how many times we choose to learn from and embrace them. How many times we choose to look for the lessons, how many times we choose faith and allow ourselves to turn to God—knowing we won't drown even if it won't go away quite yet. Accepting that sometimes all the answers won't be there, but comfort and strength always will be. I think that may be one of my favorite things about God. Not that He protects us from the blows of life, but that we can feel this incredible love and deep peace and hope in every dark moment *if* we never make turning to Him an option or afterthought.

September 2018, I turned thirty. Turning thirty I think causes most people to self-reflect, and when I did, it was a bizarre thing to reflect on. I'm amazed at myself for everything. I love who I am and I'm proud of what I pushed and stretched and tried and started and finished and gave up and changed and kept doing. I found God and the Church when I was twenty. This entire past decade is dedicated to all the things I've accomplished and embraced and tried and created and overcome and become because of merging my life with God. This past decade is dedicated to me. I really like me. And it's dedicated to my wanderings and my wonderings and my sacrifices. And yet as I think of all my trials and what I lost or left behind, even still I'm not sure I can say I sacrificed anything, because when you follow God, you will always get more than what you "give up."

What will the next decade bring? What will tomorrow bring? What will tonight, even at 8:30 at night after a bad day, bring? A new chance to allow God to show us what else He can do, if we continue to let Him. Every passing second, God is giving us a comma, not a period. I have never been more sure that it will leave me amazed and in awe like I am today, because I know God and His purpose for us.

Do you ever just stop? Just stop and take a step back and be still. And you just look around? And we see little things that have been there all along, but never noticed them until in that moment. Or we take a step back and look around, and all of a sudden, from out of nowhere it seems, a wave of gratitude consumes us, and we are just overwhelmed for where we are and what we have with us. And somehow, *we feel new*. And just from that step back comes a realization and a glimpse of a different perspective. A better perspective. And somehow, we feel a contentment that *electrifies* us, and humility that jolts our soul within us, and a resolve that changes us. *And we smile*. A real smile.

Because we're reminded that there is so much more to all this. And even the hard and the unexpected will seem exciting to us. And the overlooked and the mundane will seem vibrant again. Because this amazingly beautiful, messy, indescribable thing we're living is something to never take for granted. And we'll wonder why we don't see it like this more often. Because truly all of this is something to celebrate.

I stood in Carthage Jail. I just stood there for a really long time. I felt the bullet hole that killed Hyrum Smith. "*I am going like a lamb to the slaughter,*" Joseph Smith said, "*but I am calm as a summer's morning.*"[75] While in that jail, Joseph quietly asked Dan, who was with them, if he was afraid to die. "*Has that time come?*" Dan asked. John was singing "A Poor Wayfaring Man of Grief." Hyrum was reading scriptures: Ether 12:37–38. They heard footsteps coming up the stairs, Joseph, John, Willard, and Hyrum threw themselves against that exact door I touched. The bullet that caused the hole pierced Hyrum's face, bringing him to the ground and allowing the mob to then force them-selves in, and continue to shoot Hyrum several times more in the back.

"*O Lord my God*"[76]: The last words spoken by Joseph Smith after when he darted for the window. As he straddled the windowsill, he was shot twice in his back and then right below his heart. "*O Lord my God!*" he cried as his body fell headfirst through the window and down two stories to the ground. Willard Richards moved past flying bullets to look out to see if he was alive. Below he saw the mob swarming around Joseph's bleeding body, still attacking him, even after no move-ment. The Prophet lay on his left side next to a well. Offering his life as his testimony of the reality of the gospel we have in our laps right now. "They were willing to die rather than deny the divine origin and the eternal truthfulness of the Book of Mormon."[77]

Maybe it was because I was at the Sacred Grove when I started learning with the missionaries, or maybe it was other things, but my awe and unwavering knowledge for Joseph and his life started long before I got baptized. And even after nine years of deep study, ongoing growing love, and unshakable knowledge of him, nothing could have prepared me for this moment when I stood in that exact spot. And *felt*. In that moment standing there, I had never been more humbled and overwhelmed in my entire life.

And then I stood in the exact spot where the Angel Moroni ap-peared to Joseph Smith three times in his bedroom. Now, I know

---

75. D&C 135:4.
76. D&C 135:1.
77. Jeffrey R. Holland, "Safety for the Soul," *Ensign*, Nov. 2009.

there's a whole lot going on in the world right now, a ton of different viewpoints, a lot of passion, confusion, and so on. And it's challenging, right? Trying our best to figure out what to do and what to say and what to stand up for amidst the confusion and the hurt and the passion and the conflicting, or the tiring or hurtful or exhausting. But in that moment... in that exact spot . . . my heart . . . was beating so fast . . . and I felt my soul *jolt* within myself. And in that moment, I felt *alive* and sure and unstoppable and whole. And I *felt* that there is no way this gospel is not true and that this work is not true, and God is not true and what we're working toward is not true. It's impossible.

So yeah, maybe we sometimes find ourselves in the middle of the gunfire of the confusing and the challenging and the conflicting. But then we have these moments in our life . . . where we feel and experience . . . so deeply . . . and you just know that heart-pounding, soul-jolting, feeling is from God and from this gospel. And I can't deny that every time I have felt like that, I was living the gospel. And I was seeking after Him. Because among all the hard and confusing, I sure as heck never felt those moments that set my soul dancing *before* I got baptized.

I'm really grateful for those (sometimes rare) moments to help me stay focused on why we're here and what we need to be doing. I know it's easy to get distracted or discouraged or hurt or confused or caught up in, but I hope we always hold to hope. And I hope that we never deny, forget, or let passing time dim the reality of sacred experiences we have. And we take time to take a step back and be elated by all that we have and all that we know because of God and this gospel.

I am *elated* to participate in a living, breathing gospel that grows through revelation daily. I am elated to participate in anything God sees fit, regardless of our narrow-mindedness and personal pursuits. People say they can't believe things they don't see, like God. But I see God every day. I see Him in those heart-pounding, goosebump, soul-jolting moments. I see Him in every feeling of hope, comfort, happiness, laughter, and forgiveness. I see Him in the opportunities to change, to try again and start again. I see Him in the hard and the new and the different. I see Him in the passing time and in the quiet. Working intricately. "Maybe the trial isn't always about God trying to prove *us* or build *our* character—what if He is trying to help us discover *His*?"[78]

In 2018 alone, I was in a lot of different places meeting and speaking to thousands of people. I moved from the West to the East, visited five different countries and fourteen different states, had 32,847 layovers (*ha!*), and spoke at forty-four firesides. Just in one year. And as I think of all the places I've been, God keeps showing me that He is wherever I go. And He walks with me. Whether on His errand or my wandering, through all the unexpected and uncharted or unwanted paths. Relocating, reconstructing, recommitting, rewriting, relearning, reinventing. Breaking down, breaking through, crying, pleading, doubting, thanking, thriving. And ironically, it's all the unwanted and unexpected that has brought me to the best things. Every single time I have screamed at Him, struggling and wondering where He was, that has brought me to my favorite things. It was the exact moments I was wondering where He was that have brought me to everything I have now, and it breaks my heart to imagine my life any different.

What if we got it all wrong? What if there's something else? A something better and a something different. What if every step is the miracle? Listen. Life is worth living, *really living*. You are needed. You are wanted. You are noticed. Let's hang on, okay? Let's take back control over our lives. Let's be sick of the adversary callin' the shots and exercise our power over the destroyer of all that is good. We have a work to do, and we have a charge to keep! Let's give our life to Him who gave His life for us!

"This sounds awkward to say but, God loves me, in a sense, almost as much as He loved His Only Begotten Son. At least I can say this: He gave His only begotten Son for me. And that says something about my worth in His eyes. And my worth in the eyes of the Savior. And His

---

78. Emily Belle Freeman, *Even This: Getting to the Place Where You Can Trust God with Anything*, [Shadow Mountain, 2017] 98–99.

willingness to go to Gethsemane and Calvary for me. I'll never have to do that. I don't have to bleed, and I don't have to die for somebody else's sin, and I don't have to be that lonely. But I understand it and I love it and I appreciate it. And what it means to me is that He understands me. That He loves me. And that He reaches me. So, I can't explain how that happens, I just know that it does."[79]

Faith is not a statement of belief. It is an action word to mean that we choose to listen and act and trust ideas and paths that are not our own. It is not enough to claim to believe and to then just mosey along comfortably in our own ways. Courage to trust a perfect God is the most rewarding and needed tool to have. Remember that time I told you I was crying on the floor under my dining room table this week for twenty minutes? Well after ugly crying to God under my table and allowing myself to vent an honest prayer, and listen, and allowing myself to get up and keep moving and then getting in my car blasting a feel-good song, I truly, truly had the biggest turn around in my day with *so many* good things happening and got so much done that day! That day actually rocked. And you know, my situation didn't change at all. And you know, I still don't know any answers at all. I don't know the *why* behind a lot of things. But here's what I do know:

We are loved.

We are *wildly* loved by a perfect God. A perfect, infinite God Who is also personal.

We are heard. We are noticed. We are *wildly* noticed by a loving "one by one" God who always knows our exact situations and our exact and every thought. And every longing and every dream and every effort. And I may not know the reason for all things, but I do know the solution to all things: Him. Trusting Him, listening to Him, following Him, and seeing it all through, knowing whose hands we're in. God really is involved. He is busy working for us in the moments we think He is silent. God really is good. He really can be trusted. He really is ours.

---

79. Jeffrey R. Holland, *Like a Broken Vessel*, Mormon Channel, video, 11:36.

So maybe we don't know the *why*, but we do know the *who*. And I think that's enough. Because I know He's enough. And I suppose if we take a step back and take a deep breath and remember that we have the most all-knowing, all-powerful Being to ever exist on our side, then we can stop doubting and start embracing! And we can start moving forward onward and upward and become lighter and stronger and happy in the new, in the different, in the unwanted. And closer to Him and closer to the best things. That absolutely gives me every reason to keep going, turning to Him, getting up and smiling, and to choose laughter and choose faith and choose God, every day.

Next time we find ourselves on our floor yelling at God pleading for things to be over or things to be different, I hope that we can take just a quick break from how we think our lives should go, and with hope say, "So be it." He has something else in mind. Something greater.

And if we are consistently pushing and acting and taking that first step forward, then times will come when the scary and the hard and the unexpected turn into exciting, thrilling new adventures that come with peace. Peace knowing that we are in motion to the best-fit blessings. And we will find ourselves feeling at ease even *among* trials because from consistently acting we will have experienced time and time again that we are being led to the greater things. And we will find ourselves being our best selves, living our best lives, because we chose to trust the most powerful being to ever exist. And we'll be profoundly grateful things didn't go our own way, as we live and experience things we didn't even know were available to us.

And we'll wonder why we hadn't done better all along when we look around and see where we are and what we've gained along the way. As it turns out, with God, we have every reason to be *wildly optimistic.*

About the Author

AL CARRAWAY is a convert to the Church of Jesus Christ, writer, multi-award-winning international speaker, and author of the best-selling books *More than the Tattooed Mormon* and *Cheers to Eternity!*

Since 2010, Al has traveled worldwide, speaking and inspiring others with her conversion and faith during difficult times. She lives with her husband, Ben, and their three kids in Arizona, where she continues to write about her relationship with God, her experiences, lessons, and trials on www.alcarraway.com.

SCAN TO VISIT

WWW.ALCARRAWAY.COM